DOLLS' HOUSE
WINDOW
TREATMENTS

The Dolls' House
Magazine

Your invitation to subscribe

NEVER MISS AN ISSUE!

Priority delivery guarantees you receive every copy of your favourite magazine straight to your door

SATISFACTION GUARANTEED!

If you are not 100% satisfied let us know and we will refund the balance of your subscription

SPECIAL DISCOUNT!

An incredible 20% DISCOUNT on two-year subscriptions and 10% discount on one-year subscriptions

		DISCOUNT	UK £	US $	OVERSEAS £
ONE YEAR	• 12 ISSUES	10%	~~39.00~~ 35.10	~~80.93~~ 72.80	~~48.75~~ 43.85
TWO YEARS	• 24 ISSUES	20%	~~78.00~~ 62.40	~~161.85~~ 129.45	~~97.50~~ 78.00

Prices shown are correct at March 2000, but may be subject to change

Please send my copies of **Dolls' House** magazine to:

Mr/Mrs/Ms ....

Address ....

....

Postcode .... Tel ....

Email address ....

I wish to start my subscription with the month/issue ....
(please complete)

CREDIT CARD HOTLINE   TEL: 01273 488005 OR FAX 01273 478606

I enclose a cheque to the total value of
made payable to GMC Publications Ltd.   £/$

OR   Please debit my credit card* to the value of   £/$
*please indicate

 ☐   ☐   ◑ ☐   ☐   ⑤ ☐   Switch issue ☐☐

Account No. ☐☐☐☐☐☐☐☐☐☐☐☐☐☐☐☐☐☐☐

Expiry Date ☐☐☐☐   Signature_____

Guild of Master Craftsman Publications will ensure that you are kept up to date on other products which will be of interest to you.
If you would prefer not to be informed of future offers, please write to the Marketing Department at the address shown below.

Please post your order to:

Guild of Master Craftsman Publications Ltd

Castle Place, 166 High Street, Lewes, East Sussex BN7 1XU, England

DOLLS' HOUSE
WINDOW
TREATMENTS

EVE HARWOOD

GUILD OF MASTER CRAFTSMAN PUBLICATIONS

First published 2001 by
Guild of Master Craftsman Publications Ltd,
166 High Street, Lewes,
East Sussex, BN7 1XU

Reprinted 2001

ISBN 1 86108 189 8
A catalogue record of this book is available from the British Library

Photographs by Anthony Bailey
Illustrations by John Yates, based on drawings by Eve Harwood
Painted backgrounds in photographs by Carrie Hill

Designed by Paul Griffin
Typefaces: Korinna, Klang and Frutiger

Colour origination by Viscan Graphics (Singapore)
Printed in Hong Kong by H&Y Printing Ltd

Acknowledgements

For fabrics, lace and trimmings, 'The Dollshouse Draper'
(P.O. Box 128, Lightcliffe, Halifax, West Yorkshire HX3 8RN, UK)

For fabrics, 'The Silk Route'
(32 Wolseley Road, Godalming, Surrey GU7 3EA, UK)

For brassware, 'Meadowcraft Miniatures'
(Unit 4B Highfield Road Industrial Estate, Camelford,
Cornwall PL32 9RA, UK)

USING THIS BOOK

In this book I have endeavoured to suggest window treatments which would lend an individual look to your dolls' house or room box. It is an ideas book, detailed but non-prescriptive. I hope you will find something that can be adapted to fit your own particular scheme.

I have not given dimensions for any of the designs, as miniature windows vary in size and shape, but I have given a method of measuring to help you make and present window treatments to suit your own requirements.

Nor have I given detailed step-by-step instructions for every project; where designs employ techniques that have been previously explained, I have referred back to the relevant entry to avoid unnecessary repetition.

The ideas presented are interchangeable; a suggestion from one treatment can be combined with another from a separate design to give your treatments a unique touch. So much of our individuality goes into anything we design and make.

CONTENTS

INTRODUCTION

In the field of miniature homes, designers have become exceptionally creative and adventurous. A wide selection of power tools suited to working with wood in small scale has enabled craftsmen to develop their skills and produce some very sophisticated designs. They are making dolls' houses which are a little further from the rather conventional and stereotyped designs of the past, and their excellent models have authentic-looking windows, calling to be treated well, as they deserve.

Many dolls' houses have a front 'wing' so that the windows swing away when the house is opened and may cease to have little relation to the room. Don't let this happen with your dolls' house. Make sure that the front opening is linked to the room in a very definite way through the use of colour, texture and furnishings. Create a vignette around the window area that speaks for itself as well as connecting it with the room. It really is worth the time and effort.

I know that many people who read this book will have already treated their windows very successfully and could offer us all some excellent ideas, but to those of you who are just embarking on your first venture into small-scale design, I suggest that you take your time. Assemble all your materials and 'play' with fabrics and colours before you work on the final touches: when your dolls' house is opened or your room box viewed, your successful use of colour and texture will be spotted immediately.

THE HISTORY OF WINDOW TREATMENTS

Lancet arches in a castle wall

CONSTRUCTION

Lancet arches

Windows were once regarded as a weakness in defence. They were just slits in the walls through which arrows could be fired and smoke and fumes from the open fire could drift out and away.

Mullioned

At the end of the sixteenth century, when life became more peaceful, houses began to be built with glazed windows, using panes of glass known as lights. For bigger houses, which required windows larger than a single pane could be made, mullioned windows, with vertical bars of stone dividing the lights, were designed for both flat and bay windows.

Oriel

Decorative oriel windows have masonry or wooden brackets to support their weight and look as though they may have been added to a building as an afterthought.

Mullioned windows are common in stone churches

Dormer

Dormer windows project upright in a sloping roof; during the Victorian era they were sometimes added to the top of a Georgian house, thereby becoming part of the first-known loft conversion.

Bay and bow

Bay and bow windows project from the wall of a building, a bay being angular and a bow curved. At first these windows were a status symbol as the tax on both windows and glass was high, but once this tax was abolished, they became a standard item.

Sash

Sash windows were popular during Georgian and Victorian times, and are much sought after today. They consist of two sliding frames which run in grooves in a fixed window frame.

Wooden brackets support this oriel window

A row of small dormer windows

The typical angular projection of bay windows; bow windows have a smooth curve

▼ A typical Georgian sash window

Casement

Casement windows, which are of a very early design, went out of fashion for a while in favour of the sash, but were reintroduced and are still with us today. They are hinged along one side and open like a door.

Transom

The upper portion of some windows began to receive special attention. Coloured lights, set in lead strips known as 'cames', became popular with builders and were incorporated as small transom windows. These were hinged at the top and opened independently of their casement partners.

Eclectic

During the Edwardian era many large houses were built, with every room having a different style of window. This eclecticism displayed individuality and freedom from previous restrictions in design. However, the privilege was limited to the wealthy, as most houses were erected by the speculating building contractor from plans that were readily available.

WINDOW TREATMENTS

Textiles have always been used in homes, many in forms that were easy to transport and store, among them tapestries and embroideries. These provided some comfort by helping to keep out the draughts that came through the lancet arches. The most used fabrics during the middle ages were plain linen and woollen; decorative window coverings were not introduced until the end of the sixteenth century.

There was a wide choice of fabrics in the early eighteenth century. The whole of Europe was greatly influenced by the sophisticated designs that were coming from France and Italy, and many window treatments featured luxurious curtains, pelmets and valances. Silks were being imported from the Far East, but as France and Italy were still producing attractive fabrics, such as damasks, velvets and brocades, they continued to dominate the market.

Curtains and drapes lent themselves to even more creative expression during the nineteenth century and became a very important element of interior design; many of the styles developed at this time influence room schemes of today.

During the Victorian era, window treatments were inclined to be elaborate and complicated. Ornate brass poles were popular, and decorated pelmets and lambrequins were fashionable, but the advent of the twentieth century brought with it a rebellious attitude towards such excessive design. Some of the designers most active in this respect became part of the Arts and Crafts movement, which sought simpler craft ideas created by artisans. However, as such pieces were so labour-intensive, few people could afford what was being manufactured, and the movement was short-lived.

William Morris was a leading exponent of the Arts and Crafts movement. Amongst other things, he produced busy curtain fabrics with stylized floral patterns, which became popular in new homes with smaller windows – the heavy Victorian fabrics were being replaced by cloths which were lighter and easier to care for. A preference for a much simpler, uncluttered look was growing fast.

At the same time, an interest in all things Japanese was developing. Kendo fencing made from bamboo poles or sticks, and translucent screens made from paper became fashionable. Futons, padded mattresses placed on the floor, replaced the traditional beds, and straw mats, known as tatami, were a popular floor covering. Simplicity was the order of the day.

Art Nouveau took design into the twentieth century and synthetic materials eventually came into being – as more and more women went out of the home to work, easy-care fabrics became a necessity. Brocades and velvets, which were heavy and required time-consuming care, were abandoned in favour of fabrics that would go in that very new invention – the washing machine.

Art Deco, with its roots lying in the past, followed in the 1920s and 1930s. It derived its inspiration from the Orient and also from primitive art, with emphasis lying mostly on two-dimensional and geometric patterns in design. This, in turn, was replaced by modernism, which was characterized by very plain designs; curtains were allowed simply to 'drop' without embellishment of any kind.

Over the recent decades fashions have changed many times. The 1960s produced schemes of bright, contrasting colours on large-patterned fabrics. In the 1970s a minimal, almost sterile look was the vogue. Small-patterned fabrics also came into fashion in the 1970s and these, when teamed with stripped pine furniture, had a 'country' look – a style which was carried through to the 1980s.

In the 1990s we returned to more intricate window treatments, incorporating elements of the previous fashions and designs but today, in the twenty-first century, we have a tremendous choice of textiles that are user-friendly and available to all.

2

Tools, Materials and Techniques

Tools and Materials

Of course, it is impossible to make exact replicas of full-scale designs. The fabrics suitable for use in a dolls' house or room box restrict this, so I have chosen fabrics which give an impression of authenticity and a flavour of the period. In my examples I used cotton-silk, thin cottons, muslin, soft velvet and lightweight calico, plus some modern, sheer fabrics, along with re-useable items such as an old handkerchief and a scarf bought from a charity stall. I found them all user-friendly for miniature work, after just a little bit of manipulation here and there.

TOOLS		
Essential	*Helpful*	*Optional*
Polystyrene tile, covered with clingfilm	Stick adhesive	Modelling knife
Pleater	Stiffening solution	Cutting mat
Ruler/marked tape	Dry iron	Hair dryer
Scissors	Steam iron	Paintbrush,
Pins, needle and thread	Cocktail sticks	12mm (½in)
Tacky glue	Wax adhesive	Spray starch
Two old credit cards/plastic rulers		Pipe cleaner
Fine sandpaper		
Soft paper towel (eg kitchen towel)		
Cloth (damp)		

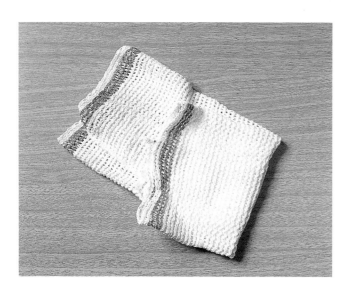

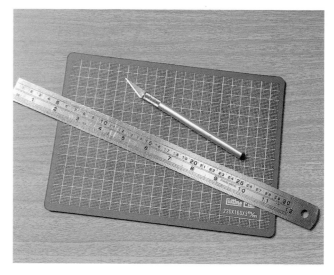

Above and over: a selection of tools, materials and found objects that are useful in dolls' house curtains

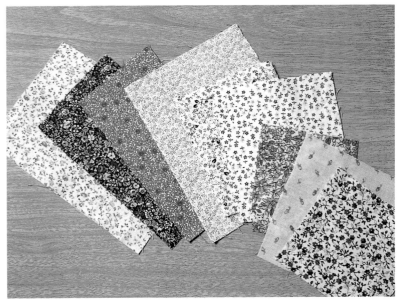

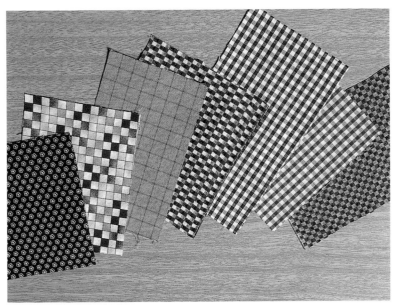

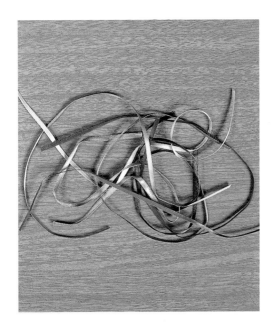

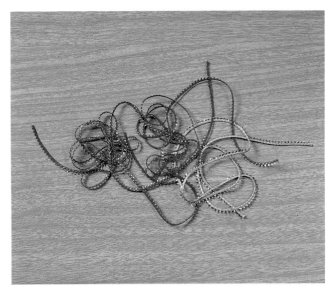

MATERIALS

Essential	Helpful	Optional
Fabrics (plain or with tiny patterns)	Squared paper (5mm)	Brass rails
Trimmings/braid		Brass fittings
Thin wood/stiff card/paper		Wooden dowelling
Cocktail sticks		Kebab sticks
		Acrylic paint
		Watercolour
		Felt-tip pen
		Water-soluble crayons
		Clear enamel, quick drying

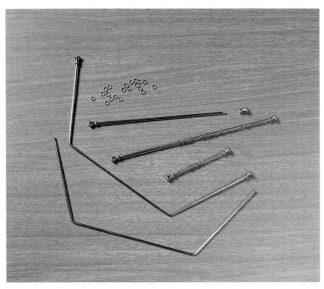

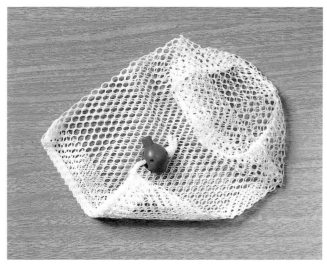

Glues

I have used two types of glue for the projects in this book; stick adhesive and tacky glue.

The adhesive in a stick glue is suitable for use with fabrics as it won't seep through and spoil the finish. Tacky glue, on the other hand, might be absorbed through the material, resulting in a disappointing finish. Certain fabrics, such as velvet and silk, do require a lot of glue for adhesion, making absorption more likely, and where this is the case, a stick glue is a better option when gluing the fabric to card or to lining material.

Polystyrene tile

The polystyrene tile, which I advocate using, is an invaluable tool – I do urge you to work with one if you haven't done so already. All my curtain samples were worked on a tile. I employed only basic tools, and much of the work was done on a tray on my lap.

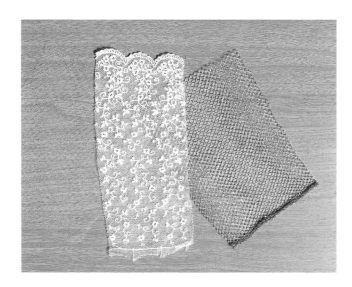

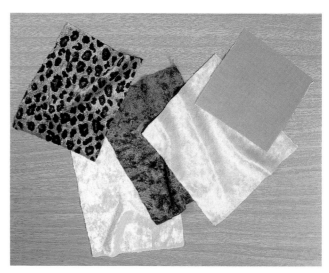

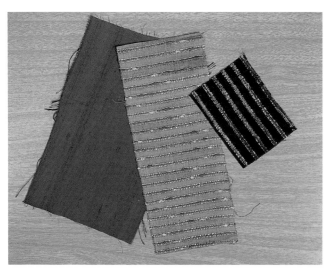

A piece of polystyrene packing or a ceiling tile are ideal for making this 'polytile tool'.

Materials

Chosen polystyrene tile
Clingfilm
Window pattern (see page 12)

METHOD

1 Prepare a strip of clingfilm roughly the same width as the polystyrene tile and long enough to wrap completely around it, with an overlap at the back to prevent it from slipping loose.

2 Insert the drawn window pattern between the clingfilm and the polytile.

3 Cover the polystyrene tile with another strip of clingfilm, wrapping it round in the opposite direction. Again, overlap it at the back of the tile to keep it taut.

You now have a very useful baseboard on which to lay your pieces of fabric and fashion your curtains to fit the specific window pattern. (See Gathering in Chapter 3, page 14.)

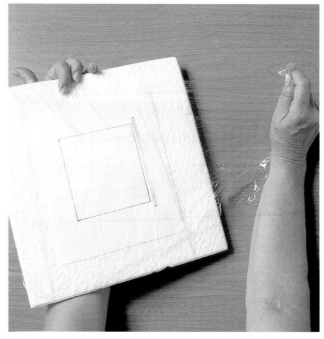

Covering the tile with the second sheet of clingfilm

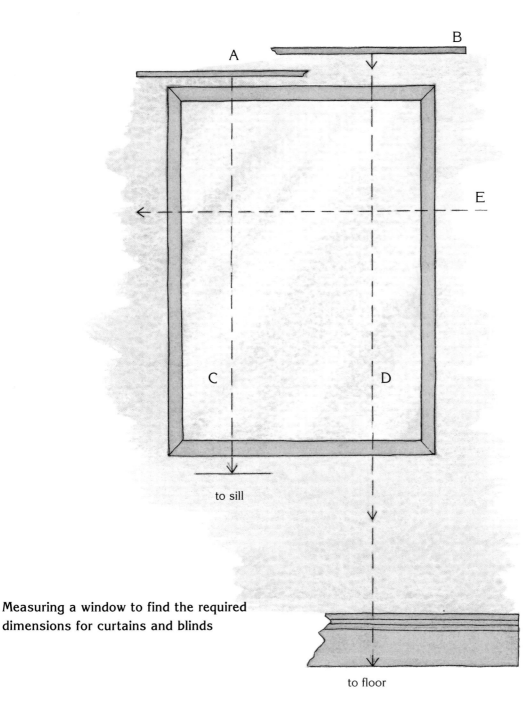

A

B

E

C

D

to sill

Measuring a window to find the required dimensions for curtains and blinds

to floor

TECHNIQUES

Measuring and drawing up patterns

I have not given dimensions for any of the designs as miniature windows vary in size and shape, but the system of measuring I have given here will help you present your window treatments in your own individual style.

CURTAINS HUNG FROM A RAIL

1 First, use a short ruler or a marked tape to measure the width and depth of the window. Write down the measurements and draw the exact shape on a piece of paper.

2 Now measure for the rail. Draw this on your pattern in its proposed position over the window. The pattern can be used with a prepared polystyrene tile (see page 10).

Key to illustration, left

A use a lower rail position for short curtains

B use a higher rail position for long curtains

C for short curtains, measure the drop to the sill or just below

D for long curtains, measure the drop to the floor

E measure the width according to the chosen length of rail, then make a paper pattern or template for the curtains. One curtain should measure at least three-quarters the width of the window; the actual size will depend on the type of fabric you are using. Bunch a piece up to get an idea of how it will behave when it is gathered or pleated

If you want your curtains to give the impression that your window is wider than it really is, the rail must be longer than the width of the window.

A helpful rule is that the rail should be positioned close to the top of the window frame for short curtains, and placed higher up for long ones (see illustration, left), but your eye will tell you what is right for your particular window treatment.

If you are fitting a pelmet or lambrequin, you probably won't be using a rail at all as the curtain tops will be hidden. In this case, the curtains can be fitted straight into the pelmet (see Chapter 4, pages 38–40).

Remember to allow for the thickness of the finished curtain top when deciding how to fix the curtain rail or pole to the wall.

Blinds

There are no rules to be given on measuring for a blind; just experiment to decide what size will look right at your particular window. The drop will depend on how far you wish the blind to be 'unrolled'.

Using stiffening solution

Stiffening solution, whether you decide to use a water-based prepared brand or one of your own mixing, such as wallpaper paste, is applied very easily and will enable you to shape saturated fabrics to your liking. If the solution is put into a shallow dish it can be either brushed onto the fabric with a narrow decorating brush, or used as a fabric 'dip'.

If applied with a brush, the amount used is easy to control and an even application can be achieved, as any excess solution can be removed from the brush before applying it to the fabric. If the solution is used as a 'dip', most of the excess can be removed by running the saturated fabric through your fingers. However, the application may be patchy after dipping, so the fabric will need to be laid on a wipeable work surface – the clingfilm-covered polystyrene tile is ideal for this – and the solution evened out with your fingers or a brush. A tissue is useful for dabbing off any excess that remains and for wiping away solution from the work surface.

A useful tip to remember is that if you dampen the fabric with water before applying the stiffener, that will help it to absorb the solution quickly.

UNSUITABLE MATERIALS

Stiffening solution has an adverse effect on certain fabrics; it is best to avoid using it with:

Silk and man-made fabrics	Fabrics with special finishes
acrylic	bouclé
chiffon	brocade
crepe de Chine	chenille
grosgrain	georgette
moiré	lamé
nylon	satin and sateen
organza	seersucker
polyester	suede
rayon	twill
taffeta	velour
tulle	velvet and velveteen
shantung	voile

3

BASIC SKILLS

GATHERING

Gathered curtains hang informally and have a natural look. Thin, lightweight fabrics, such as cotton or those containing a cotton mixture, are the best ones to use to achieve this effect. They are the easiest to handle as they are not 'springy' but will remain in the formed positions you wish them to be.

These general instructions for gathering curtains without tiebacks will help you avoid the appearance of 'sticking out' that is common to small curtains which don't have enough weight to help them hang straight. Using fabric stiffener will help with this, but it is not essential.

It is a good idea to work a trial piece in order to test the size of the gathering stitches before you start. You may find that large stitches are more suitable than small ones to produce a good hanging effect, especially with full-length curtains. Whether this is so will depend on the particular fabric you have chosen and whether or not you want the stitches to show.

I have given three alternative methods on the following pages. Methods one and two (see pages 14 and 16) are for curtains hanging from a rail which will be on view; Method three (see page 17) is for curtains which will have a heading covering the rail.

Good-quality wallpaper paste makes an excellent fabric stiffener. I find it just as good as the commercial fabric stiffeners you can buy from craft shops, and it has the added bonus of being more economical, because it has so many other uses.

Materials

Window pattern and prepared polystyrene tile
Chosen fabric
Scissors
Needle and thread
Dry iron (optional)
Adhesive tape
Cocktail sticks
Thin, wooden dowel (Methods one and two only)
Steam iron (Method two)
Curtain rings (Method two)
Decorative beads x 2 (Method two)
Tacky glue (Method three)
Dressmakers' pins (optional; see note)
Stiffening solution
Paintbrush, 12mm (½in)
Tissue (optional, but helpful)
Hair dryer (optional; see note)

METHOD ONE

This first method is suitable for fabrics that are not adversely affected by stiffening solutions.

1 When you have measured your window, drawn the pattern (allowing extra for turnings), and transferred the measurements to the fabric, cut out the curtains.

2 Place the full length of the wooden dowel at the top of one curtain and fold the fabric over it to measure exactly how much turning you will need. Mark or pin where the sewing lines will be. Repeat on the other curtain. I have suggested a wooden rail as it can easily be cut to size when the curtains are finished.

If you have decided to add side and bottom turnings, this is the time to do it. Press them down with a dry iron (optional), and snip off any folded bits which prevent the corners from lying flat.

3 Sew two neat lines of tiny gathering stitches to create a channel through which to thread the rod.

4 Push the dowel through the channel in each of the curtains.

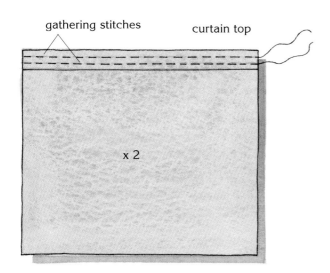

Sewing two lines of gathering stitches

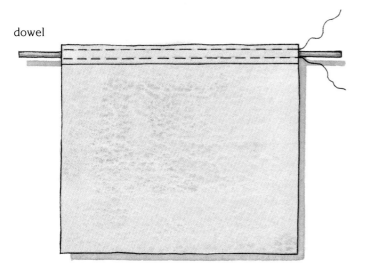

Pushing the dowel through the curtain top

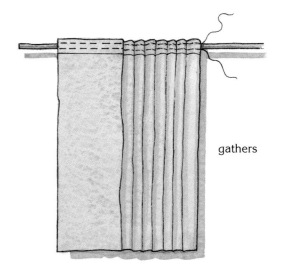

Gathering in the curtain along the dowel

5 Using the window pattern on the polystyrene tile as a guide, gather each curtain along the dowel. Do not trim the dowel yet.

6 Working with the curtains face down, which will allow you to re-do the turnings if they have been disturbed, coat each with stiffening solution. Remove any excess solution by dabbing with a tissue.

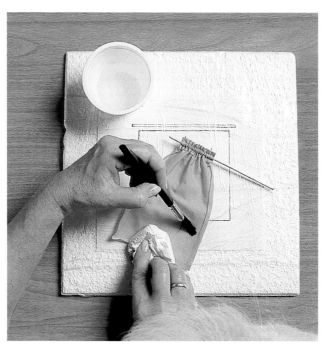

Coating the curtain with stiffening solution

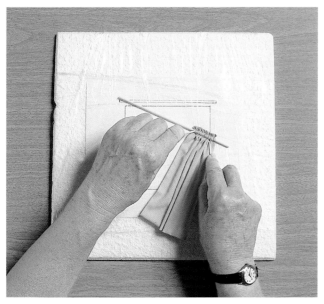

Working in the gathers

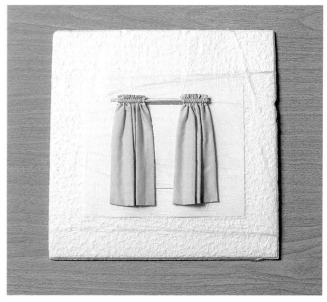

The gathered curtains, complete

7 Place the curtains in position on your clingfilm-covered window pattern. Secure the dowel in place with a pin or pins, and use cocktail sticks to work in the downwards gathers of the curtains. Use a thicker stiffening solution if the curtains resist your attempts to make them behave.

You could pin the gathers in place but I have found that pinholes remain in some fabrics, and in small-scale work these holes appear relatively large. Another factor to consider is that the pins may leave rust marks on the curtains.

8 Leave the gathered curtains in a warm place until they are thoroughly dry.

If time is a consideration, you can use a hair dryer to dry the fabric, but be careful – I have found that the air can blow the gathers out of shape.

9 When the curtains are thoroughly dry, peel them from the clingfilm.

10 Snip off any loose threads and neaten the bottom corners if necessary.

11 Trim the dowel to the required length for the curtain rod.

METHOD TWO

Curtains made in this way draw easily across the window: as there are no pulled-up gathers in contact with the rail, they will run freely along it. This method is suitable for fabrics which do not take kindly to stiffening solution, and for equipping a child's dolls' house – children expect curtains to draw.

1 Take measurements and cut out the fabric as described for Method one, then make the necessary hems.

2 Place the fabric pieces on your ironing board and pin the gathers in place.

3 With your iron in steam mode and heated to the correct temperature, hover it closely over the pieces to dampen but not soak them. Leave to dry. (Hopefully, the pins will not have left any marks.)

4 Sew the rings to the tops of the curtains and run the rail through them.

The number of rings you require will depend on the scale to which you are working. A rough guide for working in 1/12 scale is to place the rings approximately 1cm (³⁄₈in) apart.

5 After fixing the curtains in place at the window, put a decorative bead 'stop' on each end of the rail (see Securing curtains and blinds, page 20).

METHOD THREE

Follow this method for curtains which will be finished with a pelmet, valance or other type of heading that covers the gathers. It requires slightly less fabric for each curtain than the previous two methods.

1 Have ready the prepared polystyrene tile with your window pattern.

2 Run just a single line of gathering stitches along the top of each curtain, and pull them in to the required width.

3 Follow Method one, steps 5–9, omitting the dowel. (A curtain rail is not needed with this method as the curtains will be fixed in place behind the headings.)

4 Prepare the pelmet or valance (see the designs in Chapters 4–8).

5 Fix the gathered curtains behind the pelmet or valance with tacky glue.

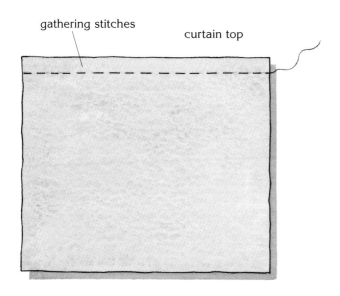

gathering stitches

curtain top

The single gathering thread

PLEATING

The term 'pleating' is not strictly accurate for this method as we are not making pleats in the true sense. However, I feel the description is acceptable in miniature parlance as the finished effect is just as good.

Curtains made in this way can appear rather formal, but they are effective in the right setting. In order to achieve really even pleats, stiffening solution can be used. However, not all fabrics take kindly to this medium. Silk and velvet, for instance, can be spoilt by its application. In addition, not all fabrics pleat well, so you may have to run a few trials with various samples to find which fabric is the most successful, and whether you will be happy with the result if you don't use a stiffening solution. Alternative methods for securing the pleats are given on page 19.

Some pleaters on the market are made from wood mixtures but in my opinion, the best ones are made from natural rubber. They are firm but flexible and are resistant to the heat from an iron. There are three sizes of rubber pleater available:

- a tiny one, which will give you approximately 11 pleats per 25mm (1in)

- a middle-sized one, which will give you approximately 7 pleats per 25mm (1in)

- a larger one, which tends to be the size most used for 1/12 scale work, and will give you approximately 5 pleats per 25mm (1in)

Pleaters are quite expensive, so see if you can borrow one for your trials; miniaturists' clubs usually have one available.

If your curtains are to be on show from the outside of your dolls' house or room box, you may prefer to use doubled fabric (two-ply). Whether you can do this will depend on the type of fabric, whether or not it will pleat if doubled, and the size of the pleater – the smallest pleater would not pleat double fabric successfully, as the grooves and ridges are too close together. The steps given below,

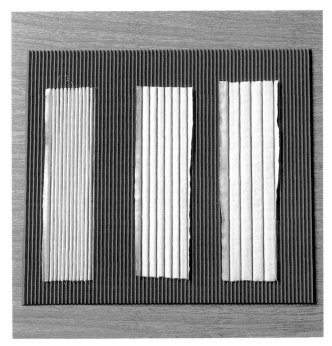

Left to right: pleating using every groove, every second groove, and every third groove

however, show how to pleat using just a single thickness of fabric. Instructions for 'two-ply' pleating are given in Chapter 6 (see Curtains from two fabrics, page 85).

I used a large pleater for the sample below. The grooves on the pleater are arranged quite close. The photo above shows the effect of using all the grooves, every other groove, and every third groove. Allowing for side turnings,

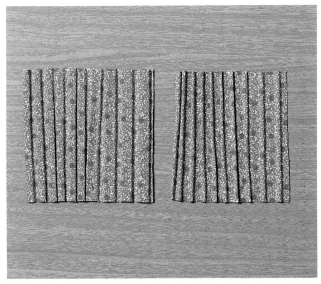

Pleating in every second groove pattern-side down (left) and pattern-side up (right)

a 'single-ply' curtain of 4cm (1½in) in width, if made on the largest pleater, will require the following width of material:

● pleated in every groove, 11cm (4⁵⁄₁₆in)

● pleated in every second groove, 9cm (3⁹⁄₁₆in)

● pleated in every third groove, 8cm (3⅛in)

It is helpful, if the hems are turned, to place the fabric pattern-side down. However, if you are pleating in alternate grooves, the fabric will have to be placed pattern-side up or your finished curtain will have a 'reversed' look as the 'pleats' will be on the window side rather than the room side.

Materials

Window pattern
Pleater
Fabric
Scissors
Short plastic rulers or old credit cards
Hair dryer (optional)

You may find that a strip of firm card folded into the outer edge of the fabric, and glued down, will help to stabilize the piece as you work, especially if the fabric you are using is rather thin.

METHOD

1 Measure the window, make the pattern and prepare the fabric.

2 If you are using stiffening solution, dampen the fabric with water to make it absorbent, and apply it to the fabric now (see Alternative methods for securing pleats, page 19).

3 Lay the damp pieces of fabric on the pleater, lining up their edges with the grooves.

Working in the pleats

4 Starting at the centre and working out towards the sides, run a ruler or plastic card down the fabric and into a groove, from top to bottom. Keep that 'plastic' in the groove to hold the fabric in place, and run another down the next groove. Continue in this way until all the fabric has been 'grooved'.

If the fabric pops out, run down the grooves again. You may find you have to do this a few times depending on how 'friendly' is your choice of material.

5 Dry the pleated fabric with the hair dryer, checking that it has stayed in the grooves and has not been blown out. If you are not using a hair dryer, leave the work in a warm place until every bit of moisture has gone.

If you are not using stiffening solution, now is the time to secure your pleats (see Alternative methods for securing pleats, pages 19 and 20).

Roll away the pleater rather than the fabric

6 Peel off the pleated pieces by rolling the pleater away from them. This can only be done with a rubber pleater; lift the pieces off carefully if you have used a rigid pleater.

ALTERNATIVE METHODS FOR SECURING PLEATS

For the following suggestions it may not be necessary to dampen the fabric first, but doing so helps prevent the pieces popping up out of the grooves whilst you are making the pleats.

Fabric stiffener
Before placing the fabric on the pleater, dampen it with water, then apply the solution with a paintbrush. Remove any excess stiffener with a tissue.

Iron-on interfacing
With this method you must pleat in every groove, with the fabric pattern-side down. Allow the pleated fabric to dry, then cut the interfacing a little smaller than each curtain.

With the dried fabric still in the grooves, iron the interfacing onto the wrong side; it will adhere only to the raised parts of the fabric and thus hold the pleats in place.

Steam iron or dry iron

Hover the steam iron over the fabric in the pleater, or place a damp cloth over it and press with a dry iron. Leave to dry thoroughly before removing the fabric from the pleater.

Spray-on starch

With the dampened fabric in the pleater, spray it generously with starch. Leave to dry thoroughly.

SECURING CURTAINS AND BLINDS

As there is little weight in small-scale work, there is no need to drill and plug holes for hanging curtains or fixing headings. Nor is there any need to consider the dry-cleaning bills or the best way to launder drapes. The attachment of a curtain rail to a window will depend on the shape of the window, whether bay or flat, and what kind of rail has been used; there are no specific instructions that apply to all windows. It is a good idea to think about the fixing strategy in your initial planning.

Headings

If the treatment includes a pelmet or other heading, gluing it in place at the window may be your only option. Attach a strip of wood above the window and fix your creation to that rather than straight to the wall: if you want to remove it at any time, you can ease it off without damaging the wallpaper or paint.

Blinds

Roller blinds, without the accompaniment of curtains, can be fixed to the top of the window frame with either glue or wax adhesive.

Brass rails

There are brass curtain rails on the market that have their own fixing 'brackets'. Some of these brackets are screw-in supports and some are press-in. If you are fitting a brass rail to a bay window, you will need to use the press-in variety and slide the rail through them before you fix it above the frame.

To do this, make a tiny hole where each bracket is to be fixed so that you get a purchase when you try to push the bracket in. A drawing pin is good for this; you can use your thumb to press it in and it won't make too wide a hole.

If you are fixing a brass rail to a flat window you can use either bracket variety, but if you use screw-in brackets, make sure there is enough space at the side of the window to slide the rail through them, as they will have to be fixed in place first.

There are twist-on end fittings available for brass rails, and they add a neat finish. Both the rails and fittings can be purchased by mail order or from specialists at dolls' house fairs, who will also advise on the best fitting to use for your particular plan.

Wooden dowel

If you use a wooden dowel as a curtain rail, give it a coat of varnish or colour treatment to enhance it, then plan your fixing strategy.

One way of securing the curtains is to fix them directly to or around the window frame. If you have gathered them with two rows of stitching, run a line of tacky glue along the top of each curtain, between the lines of gathers, and stick them to the top of the window frame or just above. The dowel will stand forward, giving quite a realistic effect.

If you want the curtains to draw, leave out the gathering thread and sew rings to the tops of the curtains, as described for Method two under Gathering (see page 16).

Fix the rail in position using a bracket at each end, and finish each end of the wooden rail with a decorative finding.

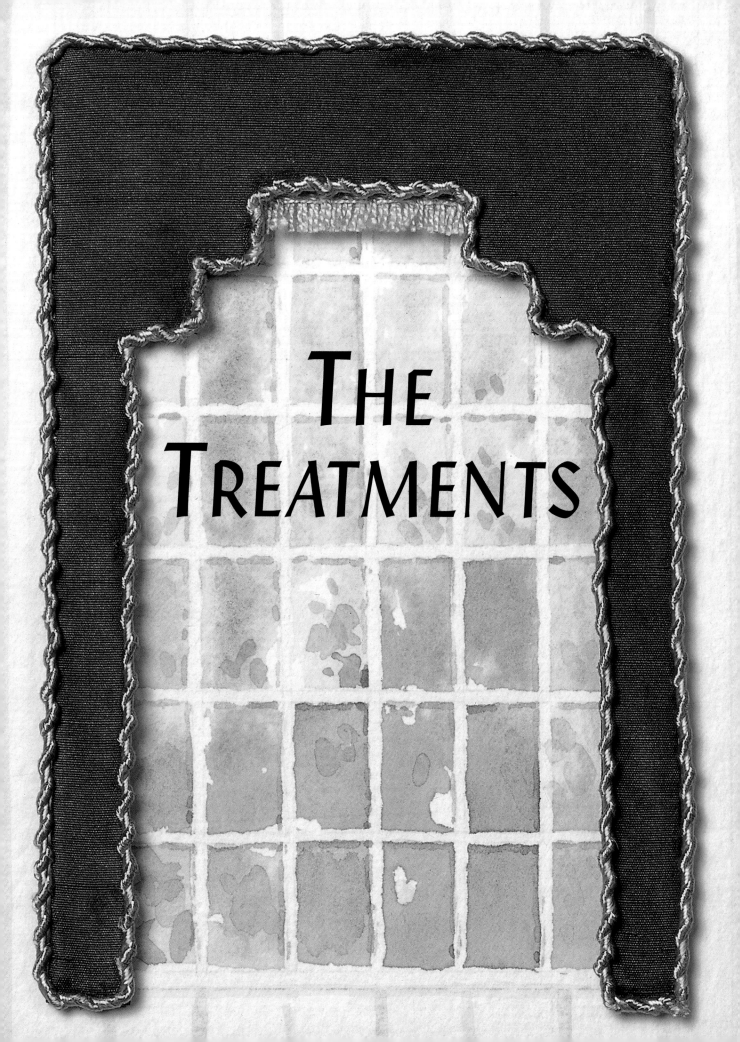

THE TREATMENTS

4

DECORATIVE ELEMENTS

LOOPED HEADINGS

This is a straightforward way of making curtains suitable for a café or a simple room setting. The design doesn't use much fabric, has no gathers or pleats, and works without the use of stiffener. The curtains hang, in simple fashion, from the loops.

Materials

Window pattern and prepared polystyrene tile
Curtain rail
Fabric
Narrow ribbon
Scissors
Dressmakers' pins or pencil
Dry iron
Tacky glue or stick adhesive
Cocktail stick (optional)

METHOD

1 Measure the window and cut the curtain rail.

2 Make the pattern.

3 Place the pattern on the fabric and cut out pieces for the curtains, each slightly over half the width of the rail plus the amount you will need if including side hems. Make allowance if you are also including top and bottom hems.

4 Decide how many loops you need – they will be approximately 8mm ($^5/_{16}$in) apart – then cut 20mm ($^3/_4$in) pieces of ribbon for each loop. Set the ribbon pieces aside.

 These ribbon measurements are for working in 1/12 scale; adjust them if you are working to a different scale.

Marking the positions of the loops

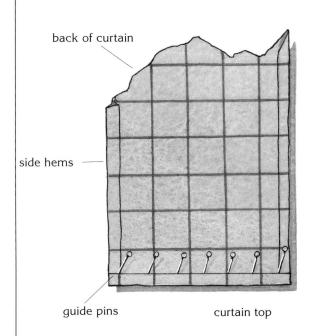

back of curtain

side hems

guide pins

curtain top

Attaching the ribbons

dabs of glue

guide pins

fabric strips for loops

5 Fold in any hems on the curtains and press with the iron. Secure them with a trace of tacky glue or stick adhesive, concentrating particularly on the top of each curtain.

6 Place the curtain pieces right-side down with the tops towards you and mark where each loop will be attached, with pins or a pencil mark, along the top hem. (Remember that pins may leave holes in the fabric.)

7 Put tiny dabs of tacky glue along the top hem where the loops will be attached, and place each piece of ribbon on a dab of glue.

8 Put a dab of glue on the fixed ends of the ribbon and fold each ribbon over, pressing the free end onto the glue, to make a loop.

If the loops keep springing apart, which may happen if the ribbon you have used is rather stiff, press them down with the point of a cocktail stick or a pin. You may have to insert a little more tacky glue. If this extra glue oozes out, remove it with the pointed tool and keep pressing until the loops are secure.

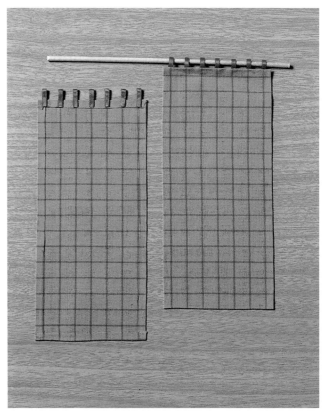

The looped headings, complete

Making the loops

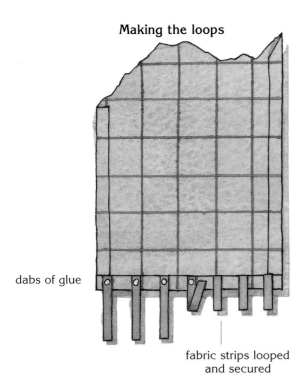

dabs of glue

fabric strips looped
and secured

TIEBACKS

Tiebacks add a decorative feature to a pair of elegantly swept-aside curtains. They can also serve the more utilitarian purpose of keeping the curtains out of the way of clutter and splash on the kitchen windowsill, when they would be more aptly named 'tidybacks'.

We can have fun with tiebacks. We can use pieces of fabric that match the curtains, that tone or contrast with them, or we can use bits of trimming, ribbon, plaits, tassels, decorative hair slides . . . the ideas are legion.

I have given just a few simple ideas on which you can elaborate in any way you please. The following style will work with either pleated or gathered curtains.

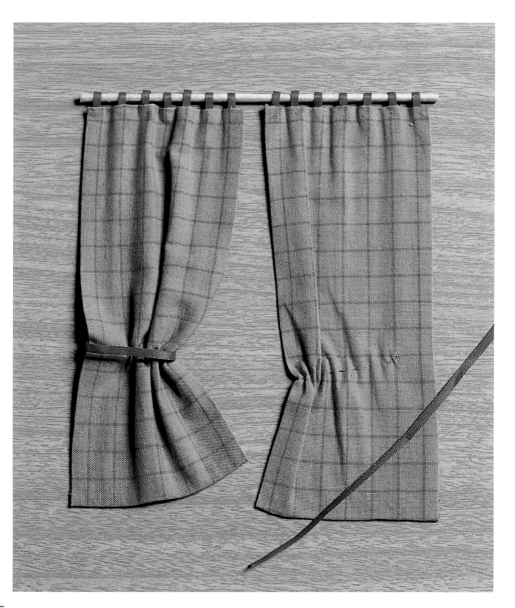

Materials

*Tieback pattern
  and prepared
  polystyrene tile*
Thin card
Fabric
Scissors
Stick adhesive
Tacky glue
*Needle and thread
  (optional)*
Cocktail sticks
*Matching beads or
  findings x 2*

**Even simple tiebacks
add a decorative
element to curtains**

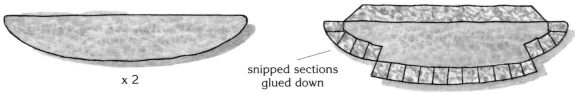

x 2

Tieback pattern

snipped sections
glued down

Covering the card with fabric

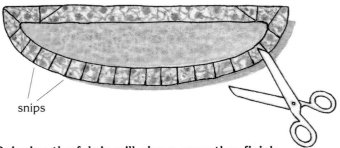

snips

Snipping the fabric will give a smoother finish

Folding the tieback in half

METHOD

1 Use the pattern above, adjusting it to suit the thickness of your curtains, or draw your own design on thin card. Cut out a pair of shapes.

2 Use the stick adhesive to bond the card to the fabric. Cut around this, leaving enough fabric to snip.

3 Cut small snips around the edge of the fabric as shown above.

4 Using small amounts of tacky glue, fold over and press down the snipped bits, keeping exactly to the edges of the shaped card. Trim off the bits at the ends that don't conform.

5 Fold the tiebacks in half.

6 Decide where you want the tiebacks to be positioned. At this point on each curtain, run a gathering thread obliquely downwards, approximately one-fifth in from the outer edge of each curtain. Pull tightly and fasten off.

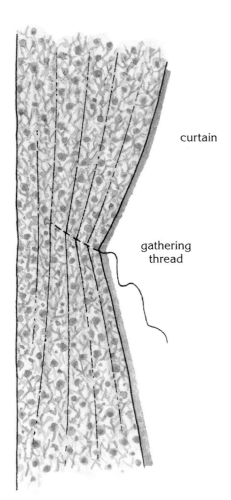

curtain

gathering
thread

Positioning the gathering thread

27

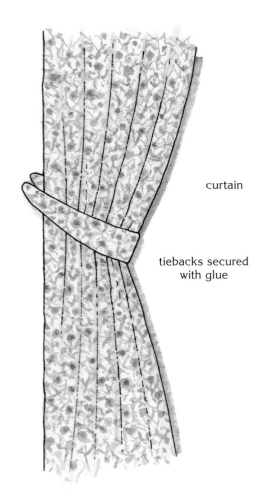

curtain

tiebacks secured
with glue

Positioning the completed tieback

*The gathers stop partway as this helps
to prevent the curtains from 'waisting' at
the outer edge when the tieback is in
place. However, you may not need the gathers
if you have fastened a strip of firm card to the
outer edge of the curtain as suggested under
Pleating in Chapter 3 (see page 18).*

7 Secure the tiebacks behind the curtains with
tacky glue. Use cocktail sticks to help position
narrow tiebacks over pleats or gathers.

8 Join the ends of the tiebacks and add a
bead or finding to finish.

9 Fasten the tiebacks to the sides of the
window in your chosen way.

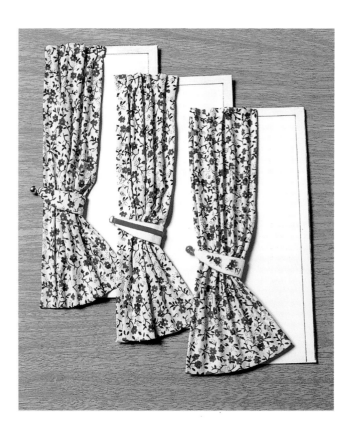

**Top and bottom: Examples of different fabrics
used for tiebacks**

ROLLER BLINDS

*These don't actually roll up and down but they look as though they do,
and they can lend character to a window either on their own or
when combined with curtains.*

Materials

*Window pattern
    and prepared
    polystyrene tile
Paper
Cotton-type fabric
Scissors
Sharp pencil
Thin wooden dowel,
    rod or kebab stick
Fabric stiffener
    (optional)
Dry iron (optional)
Hair dryer (optional)
Trimming
Needle and thread
Bead
Decorative beads x 2
    (optional)
Tacky glue
Adhesive wax
    (optional)*

METHOD

1 Measure the depth and width of the window to the outer frame. Draw the outline on paper, adding half the amount again to the depth of the window. Cut out this pattern.

2 Decide what length of fabric you want to hang below the rolled-up section of your blind, and fold up the same amount of your paper pattern. Try this length for size, hanging it at your window, and adjust the length if it doesn't look right.

29

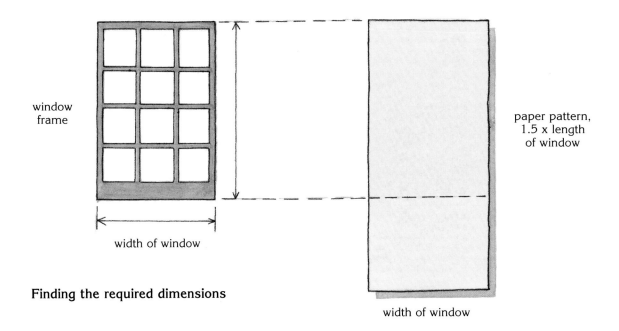

window frame

width of window

Finding the required dimensions

paper pattern, 1.5 x length of window

width of window

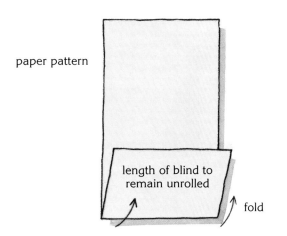

paper pattern

length of blind to remain unrolled

fold

Finding the appropriate length of blind to remain unrolled

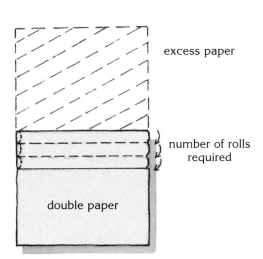

excess paper

number of rolls required

double paper

Leave enough fabric at the top to give a sufficient thickness covering the dowel

3 Leave enough of the pattern above the folded part to roll over the dowel a few times. (The exact number will depend on the thickness of the fabric you have chosen.) Cut away any excess paper after a trial roll.

4 Place the paper pattern on the fabric, trace around it with a sharp pencil, then cut along the drawn lines.

5 Apply stiffening solution.

 The use of stiffening solution is optional but it will help to prevent the raw edges of the fabric fraying.

6 Referring to the paper pattern, fold up the required amount of fabric to form a double layer. If you haven't used stiffener, press the

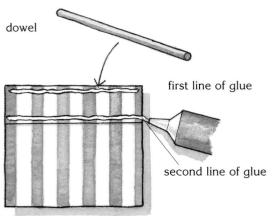

dowel

first line of glue

second line of glue

fabric-covered dowel

hanging part of blind

Attaching the dowel

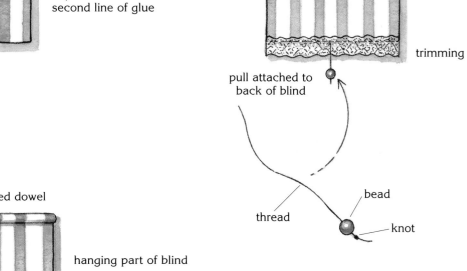

pull attached to
back of blind

trimming

bead

thread

knot

Attaching the trimming and the pull

fold with your fingers or an iron. If necessary, run a line of thinned tacky glue along the outer edges to check any fraying.

If you have used stiffener you can speed up the drying time successfully with a hair dryer – there is no risk of the blind blowing out of shape.

7 When the fabric is dry, spread a line of tacky glue along the top of the single piece and attach the dowel to it.

8 Once this has dried, spread another line of glue along the fabric where the double section meets the single, and roll the top section of fabric down, with the dowel, to meet it. Hold in place until the glue sets.

9 Trim the dowel to the width of the blind.

10 Fix your chosen trimming to the bottom edge of the blind, with tacky glue.

11 Make a pull using thread to match the trimming. Tie a knot at one end of the thread to hold your bead in place.

12 Turn the blind over. Attach the bead-and-thread pull to the centre of the reverse side, positioning it over the trimming. Either stitch or glue it in place. Blend your glue or stitches in as much as possible as they will be on view from the outside.

13 Glue a decorative bead to each end of the dowel if you are not covering the blind with curtains. The hole in the beads will probably

This blind has been finished with a gold bead glued to each end of the roll and a lace trim along the bottom edge, as curtains have not been added

be too small to allow them to be pushed onto the dowel, but securing them with tacky glue will be just as successful.

14 Fix the back of the roll to the top of the window with glue or, if you don't want to fix it permanently, use adhesive wax.

WOODEN ROLLER BLIND

This blind is made from cocktail sticks joined together with sewing thread. The width is predetermined (the width of the cocktail sticks) and may be too narrow for some dolls' house windows. A wider blind could be made from very thin dowelling, cut to scale.

Materials

Cocktail sticks or
  very thin dowelling
Masking tape
Sharp pencil
Cotton thread
Scissors
Tacky glue

METHOD

1 Lay the cocktail sticks on a length of masking tape, then fold the tape over the sticks to hold them in place.

2 Draw two guidelines along each side of the sticks – an inner, weaving line and an outer, cutting line.

3 Weave the thread over and under the sticks, along the weaving line, working up and down. Secure the thread with tacky glue.

4 When the glue has dried, trim off the points of the sticks, cutting along the cutting lines. Cocktail sticks can easily be cut with scissors.

5 Roll the top over just a couple of times to give the required effect: too many rolls will make the top too thick.

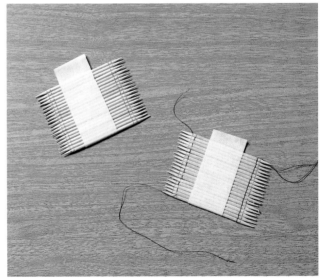

Secure the cocktail sticks with masking tape while you weave them together

6 To finish, attach a tiny piece of cocktail stick to a short length of thread to make the 'pull', and glue this to the curtain.

BASIC PELMET

A pelmet can give a formal finish to a window. It can also be a way of heading the curtains and eliminating the need for a curtain rail.

From the basic pattern given opposite you can design any shape, and the size can be adjusted to fit over gathered or pleated headings.

Materials

*Pelmet pattern
  and prepared
  polystyrene tile
Thin but firm card
Sharp pencil
Paper
Scissors
Modelling knife
Ruler
Fabric
Trimming
Stick adhesive
Tacky glue*

METHOD

SHAPED EDGE

1 If you choose to have a shaped edge, make a deep pelmet and design the shape on a piece of paper first: paper is easier to handle and less expensive than card. When you are happy with the shape, use it as a template for transferring your design to card.

2 Mark on the fold lines as shown opposite.

3 Fold the paper to give a concertina effect.

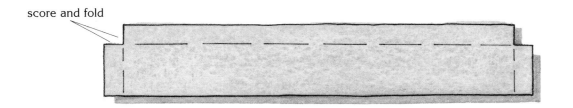

score and fold

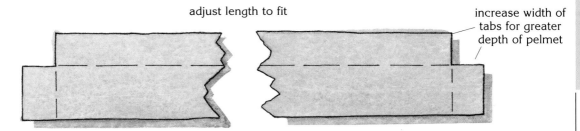

adjust length to fit

increase width of tabs for greater depth of pelmet

Pelmet pattern

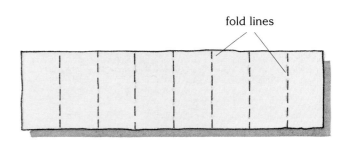

fold lines

Marking fold lines on the paper template

concertina folds

Folding along the marked lines

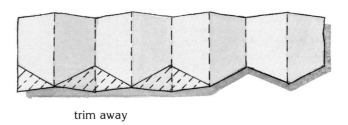

trim away

Cutting the shaped edge

4 Draw your chosen shape on one section of the 'concertina' and cut it out. Draw round it on the next section and cut out that shape. Continue in this way to the last section of the pattern. This will result in a more even pattern than cutting through several layers at once.

5 Trace around the paper template onto the card pelmet pattern.

6 At this stage, check that the pelmet will be exactly the size you need before you go any further.

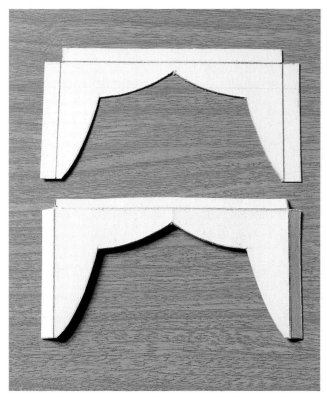

Scoring and folding the card

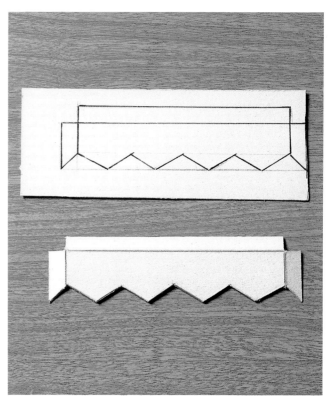

Alternative pelmet shape

ALL DESIGNS

1 Cut the pelmet outline from the card, score as indicated above, then fold the ends and the top over to form the 'box' shape.

2 Place the pelmet pattern, open, on your chosen fabric.

It is helpful to use a little bit of stick adhesive between the pattern and the fabric to form a temporary hold, especially if the fabric has a symmetrical or line design which you need to preserve. If it does, cut around the pattern leaving a generous amount of fabric so that you can check the position of the design when you turn the work over, and alter it if necessary.

If you are using plain fabric or one with a busy all-over design, you may prefer to glue the fabric straight onto the pelmet. Stick adhesive is suitable for gluing most fabrics onto card: it doesn't seep through so there is no risk of a spoilt finish.

3 Trim away the excess fabric, leaving an appropriate margin to fold over. The amount will depend on the thickness of the fabric you are using; the thicker the fabric, the more you will need to ensure that the turnings lie flat. The corners will be on view so you need to make them as neat as possible.

If you have shaped the pelmet you won't be able to turn in the fabric along the front edge, but the trimming will hide any untidy bits.

4 Spread stick adhesive evenly over the shaped card if you haven't already done so and position it on the fabric. Press it in place with your fingers.

5 Fold the pelmet over at the scored lines and join up the corners with tacky glue.

If the corners don't meet up well, use tacky glue to fix a small piece of card, angled to fit, inside each. Fix one at a time, holding them in place until the glue has set.

The finished pelmet has a toning trim which could also be featured in tiebacks for curtains

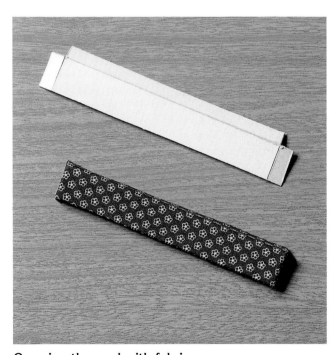

Covering the card with fabric

6 Glue on the trimming, applying a thin line of tacky glue where the trimming will touch the pelmet. (For fixing the pelmet to the window see Securing curtains and blinds, Chapter 3, page 20.)

Decorated pelmets

The pelmets shown on these three pages were made following the basic instructions given on pages 34–37.

Materials

Prepared pelmet
Fabric
Scissors
Ribbon or trimming
   to tone
Stick adhesive
Tacky glue

This basic pelmet is covered with plain fabric. To decorate it, I cut a shaped piece of the curtain fabric, following the lines in its pattern, and glued this in place. I trimmed the bottom edge with narrow braid

The fabrics and trimmings I used

PRACTICAL NOTES

The pelmets shown on pages 38 and 39 are decorated with small pieces cut from the main curtain fabrics along with ribbon, or trimming, to tone. I used stick adhesive for fixing the cut-out pieces. The second examples, pictured on page 40, are decorated with pieces of embroidered braid which co-ordinate with the velvet of the curtains. I was lucky – the braid was just the right depth for covering the card of the pelmets.

This pelmet is also covered with plain fabric. The flower motifs are cut from matching curtain fabric and glued in place. I finished the design with a length of toning ribbon along the lower length of the pelmet

Again, I used one plain
and one patterned fabric

The pelmet shown here is covered with machine-embroidered braid which tones with the velvet curtains. The depth was just right for covering the card

Co-ordinated velvet and trimmings

This pelmet is also covered with toning, embroidered braid

LAMBREQUINS

A lambrequin, pronounced 'lamperkin', takes us back in time to the nineteenth century. In its original form, a lambrequin was a piece of shaped drapery which was placed at the top of a window or door, but over time it developed into a sort of flat pelmet with long sides.

For a large window the sides of the lambrequin would probably be designed to come about halfway down, but for a small window, the sides might come down to the sill. The treatment often had embroidered or appliquéd decoration.

A lambrequin was not usually accompanied by curtains but could look very effective with sheers.

Materials

Lambrequin pattern and prepared polystyrene tile
Squared paper
Stiff card
Stick adhesive
Tacky glue
Fabric
Trimming
Scissors

Drawing the lambrequin template and fixing it to the fabric

METHOD

1 Draw your design, based on your window measurements, on the squared paper.

2 Cut out the design and, using the stick adhesive, fix it to the card.

3 Cut out the card and, again using the glue stick, fix this to the fabric.

I suggested using stick adhesive because, with other types of adhesive, there is a risk that they will seep through the fabric and spoil the finish.

4 Cut round the design, leaving some fabric for folding over. Fold these 'hems' over the card and glue in place, using the stick adhesive.

5 Shape another piece of fabric to fit the back of the lambrequin and glue in place to tidy up.

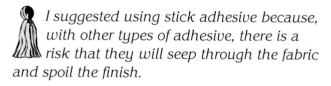

Turning in the 'hems'

6 Add trimming around the inner and outer edges of the lambrequin.

7 Attach the lambrequin to the window in your chosen way.

VALANCES

A valance is a soft pelmet that usually hangs from a separate track to the curtains, but as the scale here is so small we have to create this illusion by introducing a firm backing to hold the tiny pieces in place. The curtains can be attached to this backing.

Design one

This design may look complicated but it is not difficult to make. I used soft velvet and, because parts of the wrong side of the fabric are on view in the folds, I lined the side and centre attachments.

Materials

(for both designs)
Window treatments,
    patterns and
    prepared
    polystyrene tile
Firm card
Paper
Scissors
Fabric
Lining fabric
    (optional)
Trimming
Tacky glue
Stick adhesive
Needle and thread
Cocktail sticks
Dry iron (optional)
Buttons or
    decorative findings
    x 2 (Design one)

METHOD

1 Transfer pattern A (see page 44) onto card, having first adjusted it to suit the measurements of your window.

2 Copy the patterns B (left and right), C and D onto paper.

3 Cut them out and fix them temporarily to the wrong side of your chosen fabric, with dabs of stick adhesive. Pinning will distort such tiny shapes, and of course, may leave holes in the fabric. Cut round the patterns immediately then remove them as quickly as possible so that they don't bond for too long with the fabric; stick adhesive, when dry, bonds rather well.

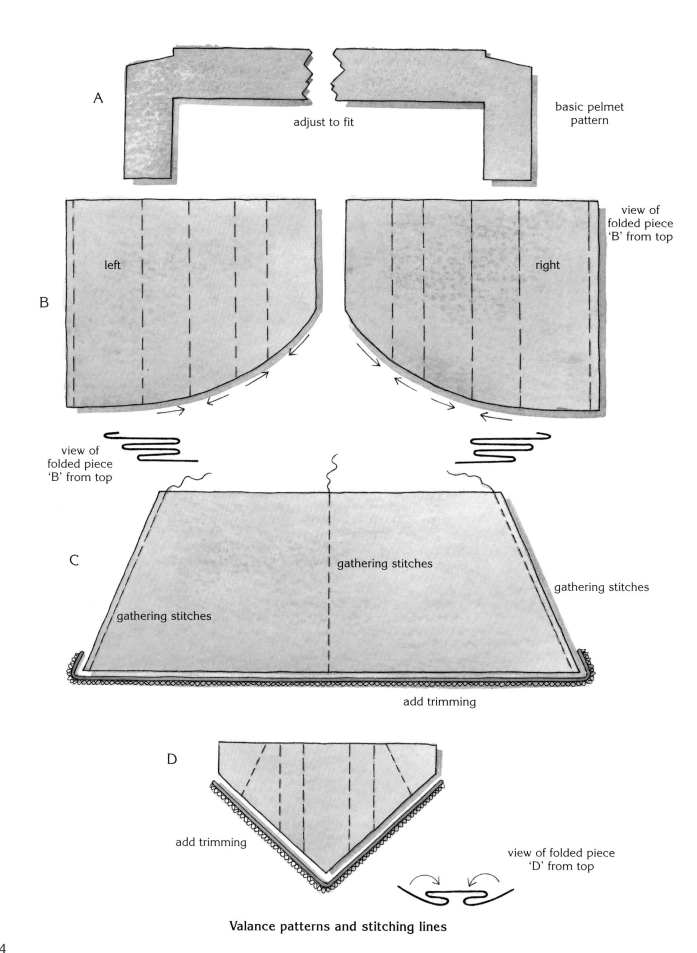

A   adjust to fit

basic pelmet
pattern

view of
folded piece
'B' from top

B   left

right

view of
folded piece
'B' from top

C   gathering stitches

gathering stitches

gathering stitches

add trimming

D   add trimming

view of folded piece
'D' from top

Valance patterns and stitching lines

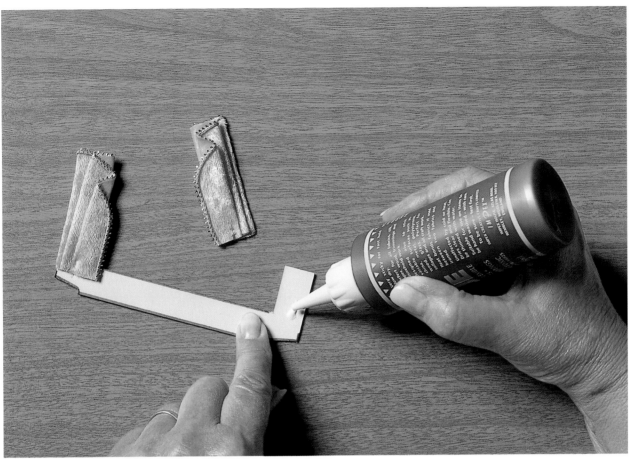

Attaching the side pieces 'B'

If you are lining the pieces B and D, then place them on a whole piece of lining fabric and use a stick adhesive or a watered-down layer of tacky glue over the complete area to join them. I used stick adhesive so that it wouldn't be absorbed by the velvet. The application of glue will prevent the two fabrics from separating when the pieces are folded. Check that the adhesion has worked before cutting round the shapes and discarding the excess material, to ensure that the edges of the main fabric and the lining line up exactly.

4 Insert the gathering threads in piece C as indicated in the pattern. Don't pull them up yet.

5 Glue trimming to the bottom edge of C, using cocktail sticks to position it. Leave to dry.

6 If you have used a lining for the two pieces, B, and the single piece, D, cut this away when it has 'set'. Add trimming to line up with the inside edges.

7 Fold each piece as indicated on the pattern. Observe the drawn lines showing the top views to help you with the folding. Press in the folds carefully with a dry iron if necessary, then stitch or apply tacky glue to the top of the folds to hold them in place.

8 Pull up the gathering threads in piece C as tightly as possible and secure by stitching.

9 Attach both completed pieces, B, to the measured card, A, using tacky glue. Hold them in place for about 45 seconds to ensure a good bond.

Attaching the horizontal strip 'C'

Attaching the central feature 'D'

10 Attach the trimmed piece C across the top of the card. As before, hold it in place until the bond is secure.

11 Attach piece D over the centre gather of C and hold in place until secure.

12 Fix a button or finding over each top corner to cover the joins.

13 Make the curtains and glue them in place behind the valance. Fix the treatment to the window in your chosen way.

Design two

This second design is asymmetrical, but the treatment could be adapted to making one side match the other. I used a cotton mixture fabric and fringe trimming.

METHOD

1 Copy pattern A onto card, having adjusted it to your window measurements.

2 Cut out the other pieces of fabric according to your chosen design.

3 Fold and press the sides following the broken lines on patterns B and D. Stitch or glue if necessary.

4 Glue trimming to pieces B and/or D along the unfolded edges, using tacky glue. Set aside to dry.

5 Loosely gather piece C as for Design one (see above left), and secure.

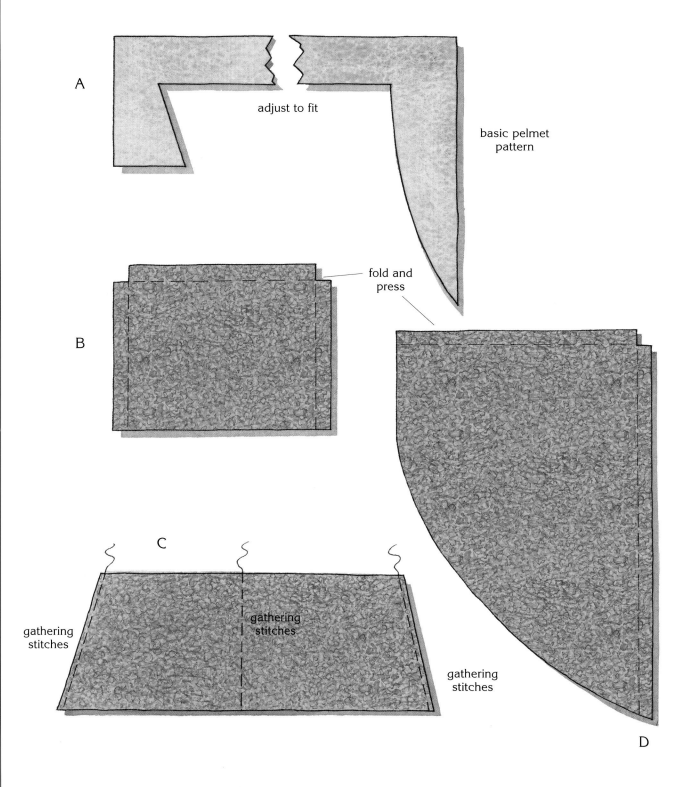

A

adjust to fit

basic pelmet
pattern

fold and
press

B

C

gathering
stitches

gathering
stitches

gathering
stitches

D

Valance patterns and stitching lines

Gluing trimming to the side pieces 'B' and 'D'

Attaching the side pieces

6 Gather the tops of pieces B and/or D with two running threads, one below the other. Pull up tightly and secure. Using two threads rather than one makes the gathers look tighter.

7 Attach piece C to the card support, overlapping slightly at the top. Fold over and glue down for a neat finish. Set aside to dry for a minute, then glue down.

8 Attach pieces B and/or D, overlapping them at the top of the covered pelmet and gluing them in place with tacky glue. Hold for a minute until they are firmly attached then glue them down to the side pieces of the card.

9 Make the curtains and glue them in place behind the valance, again with tacky glue. Fix the treatment to the window in your chosen way.

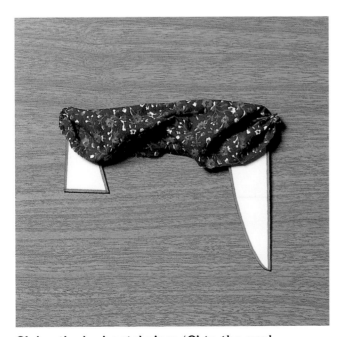

Gluing the horizontal piece 'C' to the card

SWAGS

No, not the booty of burglars, but festoons or drapes made from one long piece of fabric. Here are two simple ideas with optional trimming.

Design one

This design has a card base similar to the ones used in the valance designs. I suggest you make the curtains first as they need to be joined to the card before the swag is completely attached.

Materials

(for both designs)
Window treatments, patterns and prepared polystyrene tile
Firm card (Design two)
Scissors
Fabric(s)
Trimming (Design two: optional)
Tacky glue
Stick adhesive
Needle and thread
Dry iron (optional)

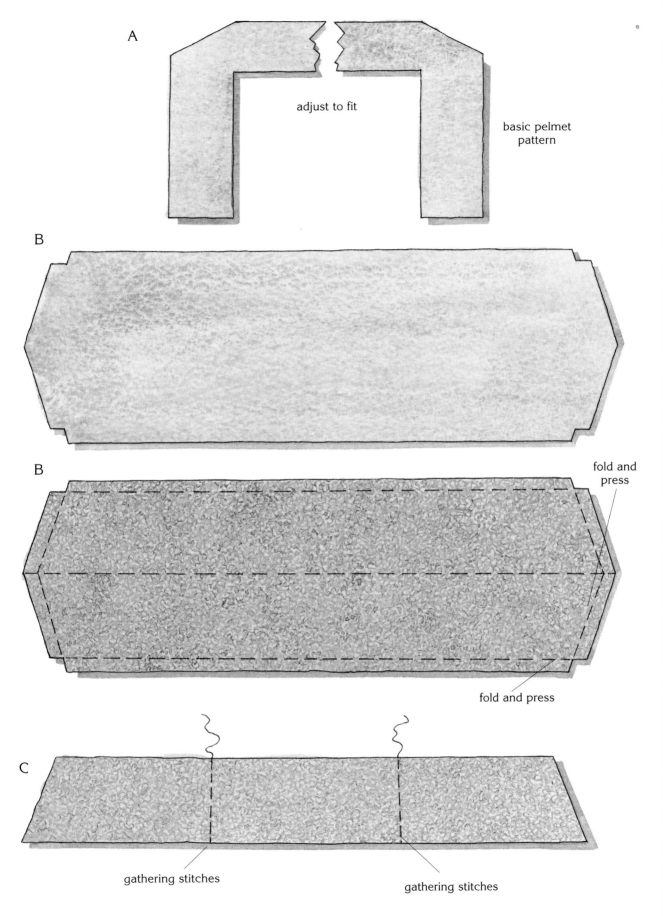

A

adjust to fit

basic pelmet
pattern

B

B

fold and
press

fold and press

C

gathering stitches

gathering stitches

Swag patterns and stitching lines

METHOD

1 Prepare the curtains to your chosen design.

2 Transfer Pattern A onto card, having adjusted it to suit your window measurements.

3 Copy Pattern B onto paper, making sure that it will fit both across the top and down each side of the pattern. Cut this out.

4 Using stick adhesive, attach Pattern B to the fabric and cut around it. Remove the pattern before the adhesive has time to dry.

5 Fold over the edges of fabric piece B and press them with a dry iron. Snip away the bits that overlap to make neat joins.

6 Join the folded-over edges with touches of stick adhesive.

7 Glue the tops of the finished curtains to the shaped card A.

8 Fold and press fabric piece B in half lengthways, matching the edges exactly. Bond these with stick adhesive or tacky glue.

9 Press the folded piece again, before placing it centrally across the top of the curtains on the shaped card. Leave an equal strip over at each side.

10 Mark the strip with pins where it touches the two outer corners of the curtains. Sew a line of gathering threads at these pins on either side as shown in the pattern on page 51.

11 Pull up the threads tightly and secure the gathers with stitches.

12 Put a line of tacky glue across the back of the swag, between the two sets of gathers. Fasten the swag on the card, across the head of the curtains, with its longest edge (the folded edge) across the top. Leave to bond securely for a few minutes.

13 When the swag is firmly stuck to the top of the curtains, pull one end round and tacky glue it down the length of one curtain. Hold it in place until it is firmly fixed, then glue the second one down the other curtain.

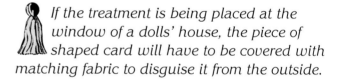 *If the treatment is being placed at the window of a dolls' house, the piece of shaped card will have to be covered with matching fabric to disguise it from the outside.*

14 Fix the finished treatment to your window in your chosen way.

Design two

This design is based on a covered pelmet, so the curtains may be made at any stage. (See Basic pelmet, page 34.) This swag is shorter than that in Design one.

METHOD

1 Prepare the pelmet, with reference to your window measurements. Cover with fabric.

2 Make the swag as for Design one, but cutting the fabric slightly shorter.

3 If you wish, add trimming to each end of the swag. (The swag in the photo above has been trimmed with lace.)

4 Attach the curtain tops behind the pelmet.

5 Fix to the window in your chosen way.

5

PERIOD AND OTHER STYLES

CAFÉ STYLE

A café-style curtain can be used effectively in a kitchen or shop setting as well as in a traditional café. This half curtain is hung by loops cut from the curtain itself, hence the use of double fabric. However, it can easily be adapted to hang from rings or ribbon loops. A matching blind can be made following the instructions in Chapter 4 (see page 29).

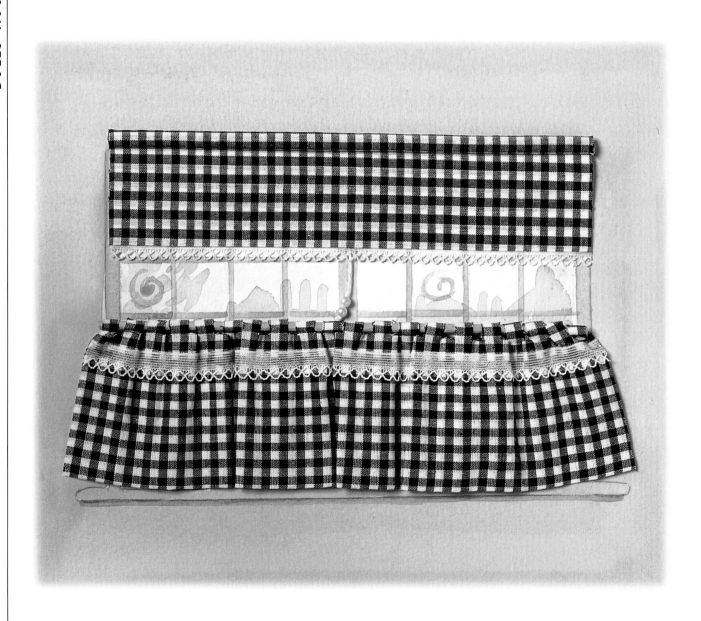

Materials

Window pattern and prepared polystyrene tile
Fabric
Scissors
Needle and thread
Stick adhesive
Dry iron
Fabric stiffener
Curtain rail, wooden, or brass if purchased in the
    correct length for the job
Fixing brackets
Decorative ends (optional)
Kebab stick or dowel
Dressmakers' pins
Trimming

METHOD

1 If you are using a wooden rail, cut it to the required length, allowing for any fixing brackets or end pieces that you have chosen.

2 Decide on the depth you want for your finished curtain.

3 Cut a paper pattern one-and-a-half times the width and twice the decided depth of the proposed curtain.

4 Attach the pattern to the fabric, using touches of stick adhesive, and cut round it. Remove the pattern.

5 Fold over approximately 1.5cm (⅝in) along the length of the fabric and press with the iron. Fold over the other part so that the edges meet. Press again.

6 Work a line of running stitch along both edges to hold them in place.

I have suggested stitching rather than gluing because the stiffening solution will dissolve the glue. Don't worry if your stitches are not very neat as the joins will be hidden by the trimming.

Folding over the fabric

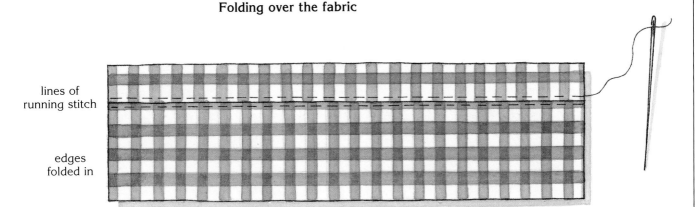

lines of
running stitch

edges
folded in

Stitching the edges in place

Cutting out the crenellations

7 Place the prepared fabric on the clingfilm-covered polystyrene tile and apply stiffener to the top part. This is so that the fabric won't fray as you cut out the small crenellations. Dry thoroughly.

There is a product on the market which is specially made for preventing fraying but I find that stiffening solution works just as well, and it helps to keep costs down if you can use a multi-purpose mixture.

Working in the gathers

8 Remove the dried fabric from the poly-styrene tile and cut out small, measured crenellations from the stiffened curtain top.

I used a gingham fabric for one curtain so I could simply count the squares, but if you use a plain fabric or one with a different pattern, you will need to make a template to use as a guide to ensure that the crenellations will be even (see Making and using a template, page 60).

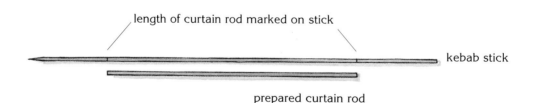

length of curtain rod marked on stick

kebab stick

prepared curtain rod

Marking off the length of the curtain rod

Pushing the kebab stick through the loops

Replacing the kebab stick with the prepared rod

9 Lay the prepared curtain rod alongside the kebab stick, centring it so that there is an equal amount of stick extending beyond each side of the rod. Mark off the length of the curtain rod on the kebab stick.

10 Set aside the rod, then carefully ease the crenellated 'loops' apart by pushing the point of the kebab stick through them.

11 Place the curtain on the tile again and apply stiffener to the whole area. Push the material up into gathers until the ends of the curtain match the marks on the stick. Place a pin between each 'loop' and even out the gathers, pinning to hold the gathers if necessary. Dry thoroughly.

 I found that pins helped hold the gathers until they had 'set', though there is the possibility that they will leave holes.

12 Glue a length of trimming over the stitches on both sides of the curtain and replace the stick with the prepared rod.

13 Fix the finished curtains to the window in your chosen way.

Another example of a café-style curtain with a matching blind. A smaller version of the blind on the café door would add a finishing touch

Making and using a template

Materials

Card
Scissors
Tacky glue
Pencil with flat top
Sharp pencil

METHOD

1 Draw a round or square shape, as required, with a straight 'tail' on the card, similar to those shown below.

2 Cut out the shape and glue it to the flat top of a pencil.

 If you need a much smaller template, for a 1/24 scale curtain for instance, you will need something smaller in diameter than a pencil for your template tool.

Crenellation template patterns

3 Place the template at the top of the curtain, holding the pencil securely, and use the sharp pencil to trace around the square or round shape. Move the template along so that the tail touches the edge of this first shape – the tail is the spacer – and trace around the shaped part again. Continue in this way until you reach the end of the curtain. Join up the missing pencil lines where the spacer prevented you from marking the fabric. Trim off the edge of the curtain if the shapes don't fit exactly.

4 Cut out the fabric following these marks to make the crenellations.

Using a template to cut crenellation

REGENCY STYLE

There was a great selection of fabrics and trimmings available during the Regency period. Multi-layered treatments were fashionable; the use of muslin or silk under curtains became popular, and these were combined with taffetas and cottons. Curtains were also dressed with elaborate hangings and embellishments. These ideas continued right through the nineteenth century.

For this design I used soft velvet with gold trimming, and embellishment cut from a decorative spray. The under-curtain I made from muslin.

Materials

Window pattern
    and prepared
    polystyrene tile
Fabrics; soft velvet
    (or other) for two
    curtains and
    muslin for one
Trimming
Decorative findings
Fabric stiffener
Scissors
Needle and thread
Stick adhesive
Tacky glue
Firm card
Paper

METHOD

1 Make the muslin curtain first. Insert the gathering stitches, place it on the prepared polystyrene tile, coat with fabric stiffener, then gather to the full width of the window. Set aside to dry whilst you make the other components.

2 Copy patterns A, B and C. Transfer patterns A and C onto card and cut out one shape in paper for A and two for B.

3 Secure the two paper patterns for B to the fabric, using a dab of stick adhesive to hold each of them in place. Cut round the patterns immediately, and remove them quickly before the adhesive dries.

4 Again using the stick adhesive, attach the card shapes A and C to the fabric and cut out the fabric around them.

5 Work two rows of running stitch on fabric pieces B, as indicated on the illustration below. Pull to gather.

6 Add trimming to pieces A, B and C; shape B does not require trimming across the top.

7 Make the single fabric curtains. Gather the curtains about two-thirds of the way down, as indicated in the illustration below right, and insert the card strips for stiffening.

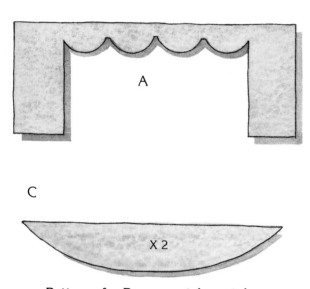

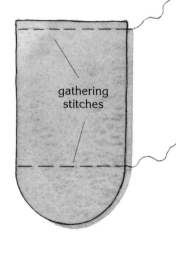

B

gathering stitches

Patterns for Regency-style curtains

The position of the running stitch on fabric piece 'B'

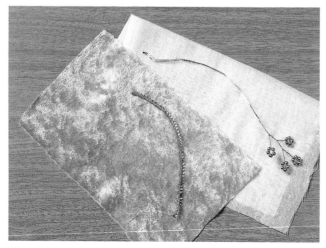

The fabrics and materials I used

Adding the trimming

There is no need to use double fabric to give a presentable outside view as the muslin curtain passes straight across the window, behind the fabric curtains.

8 Check that the muslin curtain is thoroughly dry. Attach a thin strip of paper across the gathers of the muslin curtain, at the top, and fix this behind the other curtains, across the top, with tacky glue.

Some fabrics have a habit of resisting union so the paper strip makes an excellent go-between. It also works as a real aid to the economic use of adhesives.

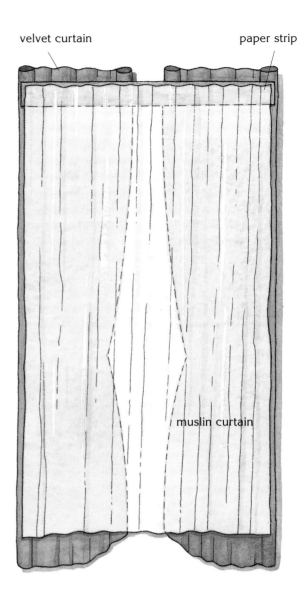

velvet curtain   paper strip

muslin curtain

Attaching the muslin curtain

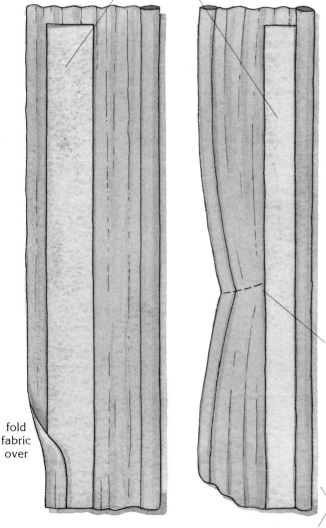

card strips inserted for stiffening

gathering stitches

fold fabric over

fabric edge folded over and glued to card strip

Assembling the single-fabric curtains

9 Assemble the components, following the finished arrangement in the photograph, with the raw edges of pieces B overlapping the top. Sew or glue them in place.

10 Add decorative findings to finish.

11 Attach the treatment to the window with blobs of tacky glue, and hold it in place until the glue is dry.

VICTORIAN

Contemporary books inspired middle-class Victorians to furnish their rooms in a mixture of patterns and colours which were based mainly on styles of the past. Window treatments became quite complicated, with layers of fabrics and trimmings. Net curtains were used to filter out the light, and rooms were usually quite dark and gloomy, with a plethora of heavy furniture and ornaments. It was at this time that lambrequins were developed.

The lambrequin shown here was formed in three parts, and for this treatment I combined it with curtains made from doubled fabrics, for an indoor and outdoor view. I used a piece of stiff card inside each curtain to support the shape.

Materials

*Window pattern
and prepared
polystyrene tile
Scissors
Thin card
Stiff card
Soft velvet or other
suitable fabric
Lace
Trimmings (fringes/
braids/beads)
Needle and thread
Tacky glue
Stick adhesive*

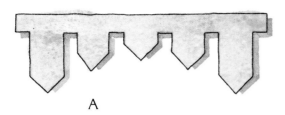

A

B

Patterns for Victorian-style curtains

METHOD

1 Transfer the lambrequin patterns (A and B) to the thin card. It is divided into three pieces for ease of handling.

2 Cut out the card shapes and glue them to the fabric using stick adhesive. Cut around them, leaving a margin for turnings along the straight parts. Fold over the turnings and glue them down. Set aside.

3 Measure a strip of lace lengthways for each curtain, wide enough to be folded double, and measure also a double width of the other fabric for each curtain.

4 Fold each strip of lace lengthways and stitch a 'seam' along the raw edges.

5 Run a line of tacky glue along the length of the right side of one piece of curtain fabric and join it to the strip of folded lace. Set aside and repeat the process with the other piece of fabric and folded lace.

6 Run a line of tacky glue along the other edge of the fabric, still on the right side, and join that to the lace to make the double curtain. Set aside.

7 Add your chosen trimmings to the lambrequin pieces. I used thick embroidery cotton and added tiny gold beads to decorate the points.

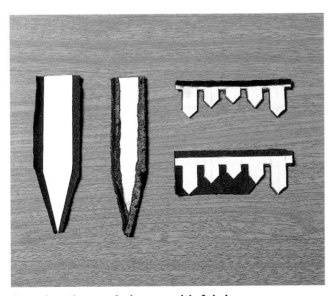

Covering the card shapes with fabric

The measured lace and velvet

Joining the folded lace to the velvet

8 Cut two narrow strips of stiff card. Apply a few touches of stick adhesive to the strips and insert a card between each double curtain at the edge opposite the lace. Gather the curtains as if for a tieback, although tiebacks are not featured in this particular design.

9 Softly gather the tops of the curtains, or leave flat for a greater overlap.

Doubling the curtain fabric

Gathering the curtains

10 Cut a narrow piece of stiff card to the same width as the finished treatment and join it to the top of one curtain with tacky glue.

11 Glue the other curtain in place, on the reverse side of the card.

 The curtains will look the same front and back, so it's your choice on which side you wish to fix the lambrequin.

12 Glue the decorated lambrequin pieces to the curtains.

13 Fix the finished treatment to the window in your chosen way.

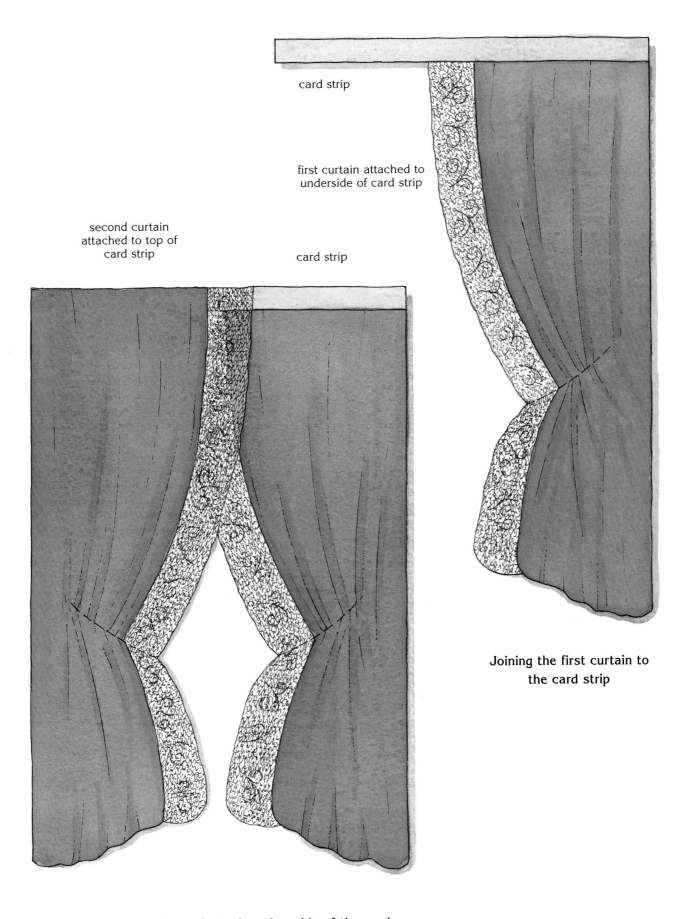

card strip

first curtain attached to
underside of card strip

second curtain
attached to top of
card strip

card strip

Joining the first curtain to
the card strip

Fixing the second curtain to the other side of the card

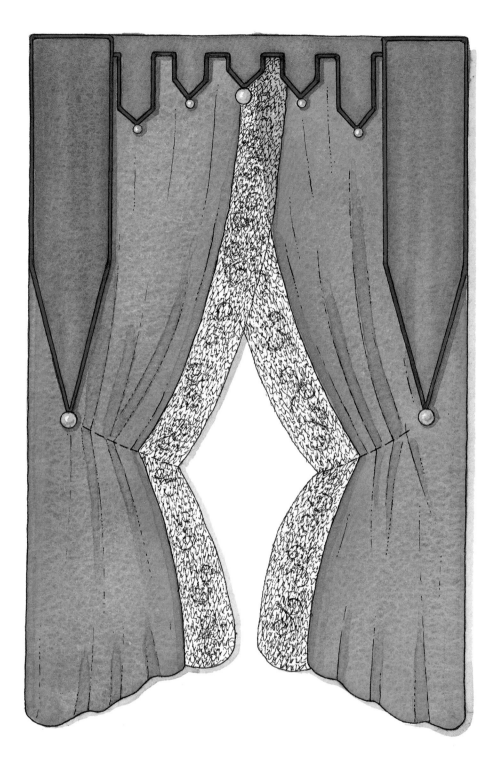

The finished lambrequin, glued to
the top of the curtains

ART DECO

Art Deco was the name given to a very distinctive style of the 1920s and 1930s. Brightly coloured geometric patterns became fashionable, and curtains usually hung straight down from the rail without tiebacks. Draped, Greek-style curtains were also popular.

Design one

This design is made from a piece of cotton fabric that has coloured squares. I cut a piece from the 'netting' bag for a washing machine tablet, and glued this to the back of the curtains for the 'rings'. The curtains hang from a wooden rail.

Materials

Window pattern
  and prepared
  polystyrene tile
Fabric
Scissors
Pleater and 'plastics'
Fabric stiffener
Bag for washing
  machine tablet
  (optional)
Wooden curtain rail
Brown felt-tip pen or
  varnish
Beads x 2
Tacky glue

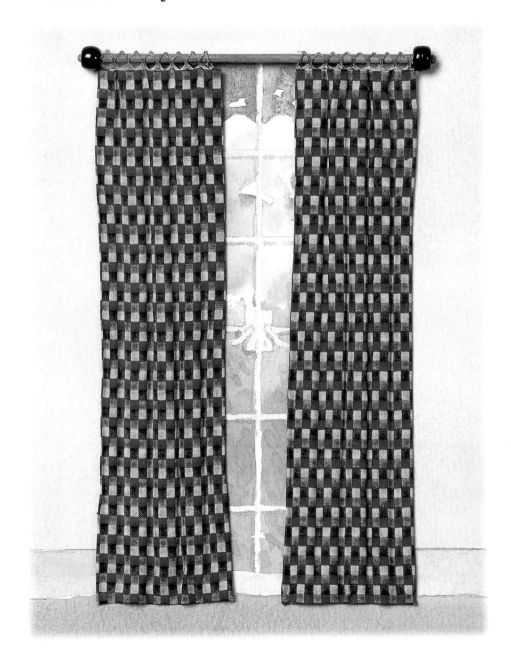

METHOD

1 Prepare single pieces of fabric for the curtains following the pleating instructions in Chapter 3 (see page 17). I used the pleating rather than the gathering technique to ensure that the curtains hang straight.

2 Cut the wooden rail to size, then colour and/or varnish it.

 Felt-tip pen is useful for colouring wooden rails: it dries quickly so the rail can be used almost immediately.

3 Measure and cut two sections from the tablet bag for the 'rings', each one the same width as the pleated curtains. Colour the sections with the felt-tip pen.

4 To help stick the sections of tablet bag down, glue a strip of fabric across the ridges at the top of each curtain, and glue the sections to these.

5 Glue or sew another strip of fabric over the cut edges of the tablet bag to give a firm hold.

6 Slide the netting 'rings' over the curtain rail, then finish the rail with the beads, gluing them in place.

7 Fix to your window, dabbing tacky glue where the treatment touches the frame.

Design two

This design shows curtains that are draped in the Greek fashion. I used muslin, pleated in every third groove of the pleater, and formed the curtains and pelmet over shaped card.

Materials

*Window pattern
  and prepared
  polystyrene tile
Muslin
Scissors
Pleater and 'plastics'
Fabric stiffener
Embroidery thread
Thin card
Tiny rickrack
  trimming
Cocktail stick
Stick adhesive
Tacky glue
Wax adhesive
  (optional)*

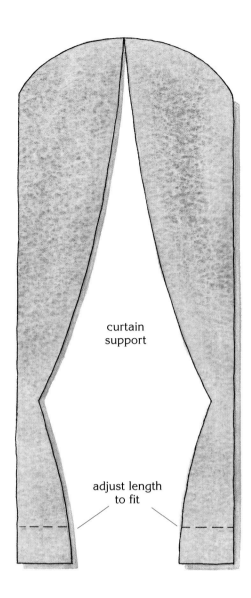

curtain
support

adjust length
to fit

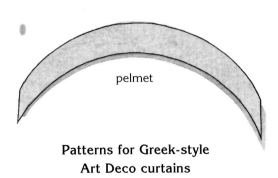

pelmet

**Patterns for Greek-style
Art Deco curtains**

METHOD

1 Trace the patterns given above. Adjust them to your window size and transfer them onto card. Cut out the card shapes.

2 With reference to your window measurements, prepare single pieces of fabric for the curtains following the pleating guidelines in Chapter 3 (see page 17).

 If you use this idea in a dolls' house, you may prefer to cover the back of each shaped card with muslin so that the card former does not show from the outside. You probably won't need to add any trimming to that side unless a great amount of curtain will be showing through the window.

3 Put a line of tacky glue across the top and along the edges of one piece of shaped card, and also across the 'waist'.

4 Place one piece of pleated muslin over the shaped card. Line up the top and edges exactly and press them gently down over the lines of glue. Pinch the curtain in at the 'waist', to take the shape of the card. Hold it in position until the glue is dry.

5 Repeat with the second pieces of curtain and card. Make sure that the card is turned the correct way to complement its partner or you will find that you have two curtains going in the same direction.

6 Cut pieces of thread and rickrack to decorate the curtains, and glue them in place with tiny dots of tacky glue.

The point of a cocktail stick is very helpful for applying dots of glue.

7 Using the stick adhesive, glue a piece of muslin to the curved pelmet, trim to shape with scissors, then add the trimming.

8 Tacky glue the pelmet to the curtain top.

9 Cut another piece of curved card and glue that to the inside of the top. This will make it easy to fix the curtains in place at the window with either tacky glue or wax adhesive. A rail is impractical with this shaped top.

WARTIME WINDOW TREATMENTS

During the Second World War if a chink of light escaped through the curtains it would be spotted by a zealous warden on duty, bringing him knocking on the door. Ways had to be found to cover the windows so that no light was visible from the outside. Many people already had heavy curtains in their living rooms but, in rooms where the curtains were made from lighter materials, something had to be done to convert the coverings into what were known as 'blackouts'. Old curtains were dyed black and used as linings. Blackout material and spring blinds made from dense black fabric came on the market. All were intended to prevent any light from seeping through, as a precaution against air raids.

Window panes were covered with open-weave fabrics or stuck with strips of broad tape in a criss-cross pattern to help prevent broken glass from flying around in the event of the windows shattering.

Design one

For this treatment I cut narrow strips of self-adhesive masking tape and stuck them onto panes of acetate. The acetate I used was from a supermarket food tray and gives the impression of patterned glass that would be used, perhaps, for a bathroom.

Materials

Window pattern
Acetate (plain or raised pattern)
Masking tape
Scissors
Tacky glue

METHOD

1 Tacky glue the piece of acetate to the edges of the window frame. The positioning of this will depend on the style of frame in your miniature house or room box.

2 Cut measured strips of self-adhesive masking tape and stick them to the inside of the panes in a crisscross pattern. The size of the strips will depend on the type of windows you are treating. Whatever they are, they must be of a style dating from before 1939.

Design two

This idea for a window design with an open-weave protective material on the panes would work in a room box where the interior only is on view. The bag for a washing machine tablet came in useful for this.

Materials

Window pattern and prepared polystyrene tile
Plain acetate sheet
Washing machine tablet bag
Felt-tip pen, brown
Fabric, patterned or plain
Fabric, black
Dowel
Bead, black
Needle and thread
Dry iron
Tacky glue
Stick glue

METHOD

1 Cut a piece of acetate to fit inside the window frame and, using tiny dabs of tacky glue, attach a measured piece of washing machine tablet bag to it. I coloured mine brown with felt-tip pen.

2 Fix this covered acetate to the window frame, with tacky glue.

3 Referring to your window pattern, cut fabric for each of the outer curtains and their linings.

4 Fold over the top, side and bottom edges and press with a dry iron. Trim the corners to neaten them where the fabric overlaps.

5 Join the blackout linings to the outer curtains around their edges, using stick glue.

6 Gather the tops of each curtain.

7 Make the roller blind to the same width as the window, following the instructions given in Chapter 4 (see page 29).

8 Tacky glue the gathered tops of the curtains to each end of the blind.

9 If possible, fold back the curtains a little to show the linings.

You may not feel the need to line the curtains at all if you aren't going to have the curtain backs on show. The blackout blind and the design of your wartime room will create the right impression.

10 Attach the curtains and the blind to the window with touches of tacky glue.

Minimalist curtains

Nothing could provide a greater contrast than black and white; in combination they can look very effective. My example uses muslin for the outer curtains and an old handkerchief for the thin cotton inner ones (part of which is also used in the Japanese blind shown on page 77).

Materials

*Window pattern
and prepared
polystyrene tile
Muslin
Very thin cotton
(a handkerchief
is ideal)
Fabric stiffener
Scissors
Dry iron (optional)
Tacky glue
Needle and thread
Trimming
Brass curtain rail
with fittings
Brass fixing brackets
(optional)*

METHOD

1 Referring to your window measurements, cut out the fabric for both sets of curtains.

2 Apply fabric stiffener to the muslin. Smooth the fabric out on the prepared polytile and leave to dry.

3 Fold over and press in hems on all four sides of each muslin and each cotton piece.

4 Using your fingers, press both the muslin and the handkerchief into folds.

5 For each curtain, lay the muslin over to one side of the handkerchief, overlapping the muslin a little so that it can be folded over and glued to the back of the handkerchief.

6 Stitch the two fabrics together across the top, catching the folds to hold them in place. Use a few touches of tacky glue to join any places that are not lying as flat as you wish.

7 Run a gathering thread through each cotton curtain where the tiebacks will be.

8 Glue or stitch pieces of trimming to the finished curtains for the tiebacks.

9 Sew on the curtain rings, spacing them evenly and matching the spacing to your scale.

10 Fix the rail to the window by using either brass brackets (see Brass rails under Securing curtains and blinds, page 20) or tacky glue, applying small dots of glue where the treatment touches the frame.

SMALL AND SIMPLE TREATMENTS

I used just a single piece of the fabric for the designs given here, otherwise the basic process for making these blinds, and for fixing them to a window, is the same as that given for the Roller blind in Chapter 4 (see page 29).

Japanese blind

I made this blind from a leftover piece of the cotton handkerchief I used for the minimalist curtains shown on page 75. The bottom of the blind is the woven border of the handkerchief, turned under to form a small hem.
The Japanese writing reads 'long life' and 'happiness'.

Materials

Window pattern
   and prepared
   polystyrene tile
Thin cotton fabric
   (a handkerchief
   is ideal)
Scissors
Needle and thread
Tiny black beads x 3
Dowel
Fabric stiffener
Dry iron
Tacky glue
Paper
Italic pen, black

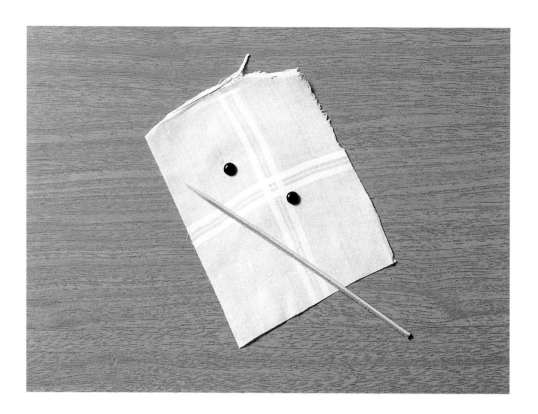

The fabric and trimmings I used

PRACTICAL NOTES

I copied the writing from a photograph onto paper. My fabric was thin enough to see through, so I traced it from this straight onto the blind, with an italic pen. If your fabric is thin enough, you could trace this writing directly onto it; if not, you'll have to copy it freehand.

Each end of the roll is finished with a flat black bead, and the 'pull' is a string threaded with three tiny black beads.

Because the fabric was so soft, I treated it with stiffener and, when it was almost dry, pressed it with an iron. This made it quite stiff and stable enough to write on without the ink running and ruining the finished effect.

Sari blind

*I call this a 'sari blind' because the lovely ribbon, from which
it is made, is very like the border on a sari that a friend bought for me
in Bangladesh. The ribbon is fairly rigid but it wasn't
difficult to work with.*

Materials

*Gift ribbon
Scissors
Cocktail stick
  or dowel
Tacky glue
Large-holed
  gilt beads x 2*

The sari blind 'ingredients'

PRACTICAL NOTES

Because the width of the blind is pre-determined by the width of your ribbon, this treatment is not suitable for a wider window. However, you might be able to join a number of ribbon sections together to increase your blind's final width.

The ribbon I used fitted perfectly across a cocktail stick; all I did to finish was fix a large-holed gilt bead over each end. Alternatively, you could just chop off the points of the stick when the glued roll has set.

Sun blind

Several of these sun blinds could look quite effective in a conservatory, especially if each one was 'pulled up' to a different height from its neighbour.

Materials

Window pattern and prepared polystyrene tile
Thin cotton fabric (a handkerchief is ideal)
Dowel
Scissors
Pleater
Fabric stiffener (optional)
Hair dryer (optional)
Trimming
Needle and thread
Decorative bead

PRACTICAL NOTES

This blind is made from a single piece of cotton fabric which I stiffened and pleated horizontally. I added a strip of decorative trimming to the bottom of the blind, and a pull made from a bead knotted onto a small length of thread.

Country-style pelmet and curtain

*There are big and small country houses but visions of country living,
for most, conjure up the mental picture of a farmhouse or cottage from
a bygone era. The method for making this pelmet and curtain is the
same as Method one under Gathering in Chapter 3 (see page 14).*

Materials

*Window pattern
    and prepared
    polystyrene tile
Thin cotton fabric
    (a handkerchief
    is ideal)
Calico or muslin
Scissors
Dowel
Tacky glue
Needle and thread
Fabric stiffener
Hair dryer (optional)
Cocktail sticks or
    toothpicks x 2
Dirty water*

PRACTICAL NOTES

This idea could be characteristic of a busy farmhouse or cottage kitchen. It consists of a frilled pelmet and a half curtain.

The half curtain has the distressed look of a curtain that has led a very full life, soaking up water from potted plants, absorbing condensation and dust, catching splashes from the washing up, and being constantly moved aside to make more space for the usual windowsill clutter. Both the frilled pelmet and the half curtain were made from muslin which I gathered onto pieces of wooden dowel and then stiffened. I added a little drop of thinned 'dirty' water to give the distressed marks.

To fix the pelmet and curtain to the window, trim the pieces of dowel up to the edges of the fabrics, then apply tacky glue to both treatments where they will touch the window frame, and fix in place.

6

DESIGN SCHEMES

CURTAINS FROM TWO FABRICS

Curtains made from two different fabrics can add a new dimension
to a room design. Fabrics which co-ordinate well and are
easy to handle are suitable for these ideas.

Design one

This uses both pleating and gathering techniques; the doubled fabric
gives a neat appearance from the inside and the outside of the window.
I have used cotton, combining checks with a design of tiny leaves.

Materials

Window pattern
  and prepared
  polystyrene tile
Scissors
Fabrics x 2
Pleater
Curtain rail
Stiffening solution
  (optional)
Tissue
Dry iron
Needle and thread
Stick adhesive
Tacky glue
Narrow ribbon

METHOD

1 Measure enough of the fabric for each pleated curtain to fold to the centre in order to double over as shown in the illustration below. Press with a dry iron.

2 Place the folded pieces on the pleater, lining up the sides with the grooves.

3 Dampen the folded pieces, first with water and then with stiffening solution, if you have chosen to use it (see Pleating in Chapter 3, page 17). Make sure that the water and solution penetrates the double layer of fabric. Dab off excess moisture with a tissue.

4 Work in the pleats, following the process given in Chapter 3 (see page 17), then set the work aside to dry.

Working in the pleats

5 Cut out two single pieces of the contrasting fabric, making them about five-sixths the length of the pleated curtains. Double fabric is not necessary for this part of the design.

6 Turn up and press all the edges, for hems, then secure them with stick adhesive.

7 Gather the tops of the curtains and, if you wish, work a line of gathering stitches in the position where the tiebacks will go (see Gathering in Chapter 3, page 14).

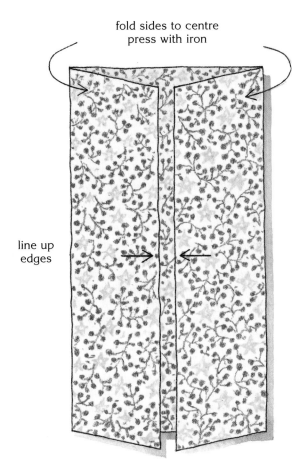

fold sides to centre
press with iron

line up
edges

**Folding the edges of the
fabric over**

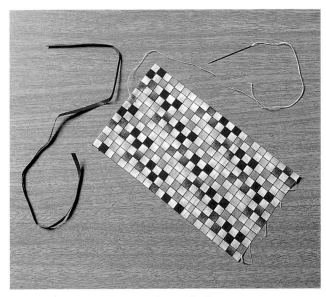

Working a line of gathering stitch

8 Add ribbon trimming and tiebacks.

9 Use a little tacky glue to fix the pleated curtains a little way down the gathered ones, leaving the top free to take the curtain rail.

10 Thread the rail through the curtains, or glue it to the back of their gathered tops.

11 Fix the finished treatment to the window in your chosen way.

Design two

This design combines a plain fabric, polyester with a slub in the treatment shown, with a floral cotton print. The 'pelmet' is simply a straight piece of covered card, but it could be adapted (see Basic pelmet in Chapter 4, page 34). All the fabric pieces, except for that covering the pelmet, are double.

Materials

Window pattern and prepared polystyrene tile
Fabrics x 2
Scissors
Dry iron
Firm card
Needle and thread
Stick adhesive
Tacky glue

METHOD

1 Turn up and press the sides and bottom hems of the pieces of plain fabric.

2 Turn up a hem along the bottom of each piece of patterned fabric and press them in half lengthways.

3 Use the stick adhesive to join a patterned and a plain piece together, along their length, for each curtain.

4 Cut a strip of card for the pelmet, then cut a piece of plain fabric to cover this. Fix the fabric in place with tacky glue.

5 Use a piece of double fabric to make the frill and gather it quite tightly (see Gathering in Chapter 3, page 14). Tacky glue it to the pelmet card.

6 Glue the assembled curtains to the back of the pelmet, again using tacky glue.

7 Measure and cut a strip of wood to fit inside the pelmet. Tacky glue this to the wall, just above the window frame, and attach the pelmet over this, again with tacky glue. Place small blobs of glue on the window frame in places where the curtains need to touch it for a good effect, and press to fix in place.

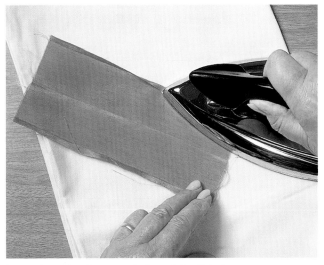

Pressing the hems of the plain fabric

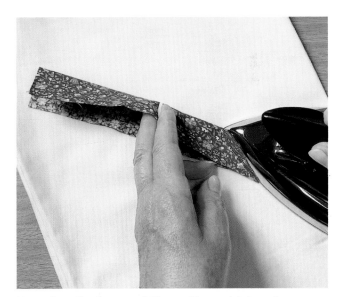

Pressing the hems of the patterned trimmings

Gluing the two fabrics together

LINKING TWO WINDOWS

An interesting effect can be achieved when two windows are linked together by a shared rail, pelmet or valance. A table or desk could be placed between the windows.

Design one

This design makes the window wall look wider than it is, with the shared pelmet covered to match the outer curtains.

PRACTICAL NOTES

This treatment has two patterned outer curtains which are pleated, and two inner curtains which are gathered. It is made following the same basic method as that given for Design two under Curtains from two fabrics (see page 87). The tiebacks and pelmet use the same fabric as the outer curtains. (See Tiebacks and Basic pelmet in Chapter 4, pages 26 and 34.) I treated both sets of curtains with fabric stiffener.

Design two

This treatment incorporates straight lines with seemingly soft curves in an Art Deco fashion. The curtains hang from rings on a shared brass rail.

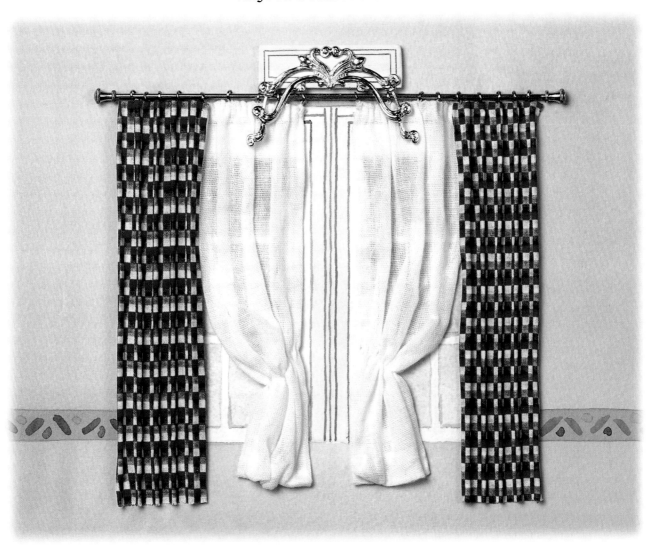

PRACTICAL NOTES

For this idea I combined the geometrical Art Deco look with the Greek-style draped one. As for Design one, the outer curtains are pleated and the inner ones gathered, and both fabrics are treated with stiffener. The use of stiffener, of course, is entirely optional. You may prefer to use one of the other techniques suggested under Pleating, in Chapter 3 (see page 17).

This set of curtains hangs from brass rings threaded over a brass rail. The decoration, which spans the centre of the rail, is a finding. The small piece of acrylic-painted wood behind the decoration lifts it out to the same level as the rail.

The lines drawn between and beneath the windows pick up the colours in the patterned curtains. These lines, which are repeated on the painted wood above the rail, are part of the composite design. To use this idea, measure the distance between your windows and draw the lines on paper. This paper can then be pasted onto the wall as part of the link.

89

CO-ORDINATED CURTAINS AND BLINDS

*Here are two ideas for co-ordinating curtains and blinds.
I have used contrasting fabrics and moved away from more
conventional window treatments.*

Design one

*This design uses a different fabric for each curtain and
has a blind which combines the two.*

Materials

(for both designs)
*Window pattern
and prepared
polystyrene tile*
*Fabrics x 2 (one
plain, one with
outlined patterns)*
*Fabric stiffener
(optional)*
Dry iron
Dowel
Sharp pencil
Paper
*Stick adhesive
(Design one)*
Scissors
Tacky glue
*Trimming
(Design one)*
Needle and thread
Bead

Gluing the shaped, patterned fabric to the plain one

METHOD

1 Make gathered or pleated curtains (see Gathering or Pleating in Chapter 4, page 14 or 17). Set them aside to dry if you use stiffener.

2 Following the instructions given for measuring in Roller blinds (see Chapter 4, page 29), cut out the plain fabric.

3 Cut a shaped piece from the patterned fabric, following the outlines in the pattern, about one-third the size of the plain piece cut for the blind. Using stick adhesive, glue this to the bottom third of the plain fabric.

4 Cut another piece, this time unshaped, and glue it to the top third. Check that the fabrics have bonded satisfactorily.

5 Fold the bottom third up, keeping the patterned fabric facing out, and press.

6 Cut the dowel to size, and glue it across the top of the blind.

7 With the dowel and the shaped fabric facing up, apply a line of tacky glue just above the shaped, patterned fabric. Roll the dowel down to this line and hold in place to secure.

8 Finish the blind with trimming and a pull.

 I used a lace trim and ran a matching piece down the edge of the plain curtain.

Gluing the unshaped fabric to the plain fabric

9 Assemble the curtains and blind. I didn't include a curtain rail, but simplified the assembly by fixing the curtains to the front of the blind with tacky glue.

10 Fix to the window in your chosen way when all the pieces are secure.

Gluing the dowel to the top of the blind

Rolling down the dowel to cover it with fabric

Design two

For this design I used gingham and floral patterns to demonstrate how two unrelated fabrics can be linked. The single fabric curtains are tightly gathered and stiffened.

METHOD

1 Cut fabric pieces for the two curtains. Turn and press the side hems.

2 Cut the contrasting fabric for the curtain trims, allowing enough for doubling. Turn up the hems on both pieces, then fold them in half and press before attaching the trims to the bottom of the curtains with tacky glue.

3 Gather the curtains on the polystyrene tile (see Gathering in Chapter 3, page 14).

4 Make the blind following the instructions given for Roller blind in Chapter 4 (see page 29), using the same fabric as for the curtain trim.

5 Make a trim for the blind from the fabric that you used for the curtains. Attach it to the bottom of the blind.

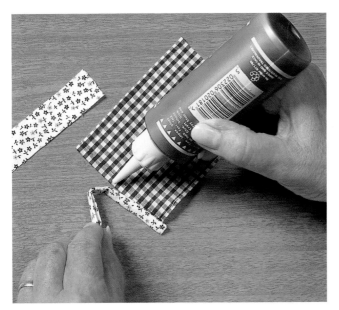

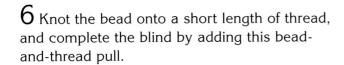

Attaching the trimming to the curtain bottom

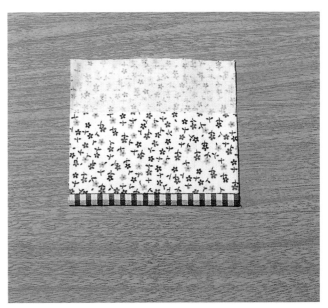

Attaching the trimming to the bottom of the blind

6 Knot the bead onto a short length of thread, and complete the blind by adding this bead-and-thread pull.

7 Cut some flowers from the floral fabric and glue them randomly to each curtain checking

first, if you have used stiffening solution, that the curtains are completely dry.

8 Assemble the window treatment using tacky glue. Fix it to the window in your chosen way when all the pieces are secure.

7

ROOM SETTINGS

NURSERY IDEAS

Victorian nurseries were usually devoid of window coverings.
Draperies were considered to be a health risk in areas that were
frequented by young children, presumably because of the
amount of dust they harboured.

Design one

This could be made to fit in with any nursery décor (except Victorian) as
it is quite conventional and isn't strongly reminiscent of any particular
era. It consists of tulle curtains with tiebacks to match the pretty fabric
blind. The curtains, which could be made of lace, hang from a brass rail.

Materials

Window pattern
  and prepared
  polystyrene tile
Tulle or fine lace
Pins
Fabric
Sharp scissors
Fabric stiffener
  (optional)
Dowel
Dry iron
Tacky glue
Stick adhesive
Needle and thread
Trimming
Curtain rail
Brass beads x 3 (plus
  2 beads or findings
  for the ends if you
  are using a wooden
  rail; brass rails will
  have ends)

METHOD

1 With reference to your window pattern, prepare the pieces of tulle. Cut two pieces, each one slightly larger than you require. Place them together, one over the other, on your prepared polytile, with your window pattern in position. Secure the tulle with pins, using as many as you need to hold it still while you cut it to size: tulle has a habit of 'jumping' away from scissors, so it needs to be held very firmly.

2 Using very sharp scissors, slowly cut through both pieces of tulle at the same time. Discard the offcuts and remove the pins and pieces of tulle from the polytile.

3 Fold over the top of each piece of tulle to give enough depth to run two gathering threads across it. Pin the folds to hold them in position.

4 Run two gathering threads along the top of each curtain, placing them wide enough apart to insert the rail between them.

5 Insert the rail and pull up the gathering threads, securing them with stitches.

 I didn't make any other turnings on the curtains as they would have shown and spoilt the 'sheer' look of the fabric.

6 Make the blind following the instructions given for Roller blind in Chapter 4, adding trimming along the bottom (see page 29).

7 Fold and press long pieces of matching fabric into narrow strips for the tiebacks.

8 Attach a bead-and-thread pull to the blind.

9 Sew a bead to each of the tiebacks.

10 Gather up the curtains by hand (there is no need to work any gathering stitches) and attach the tiebacks by wrapping them around the curtains and then stitching them in place.

11 Fix the brass endings or matching beads at each end of the rail. My curtains hang from a brass rail which has its own screw ends.

12 Assemble the treatment by using tacky glue to fix the blind in position behind the tops of the curtains, with the roll just under the curtain rail.

13 You could use bracket fittings to fix the brass rail to the window or, alternatively, you could run a line of tacky glue behind the rolled top of the blind and secure it in that way. Tacky glue will support the treatment for either the brass or the wooden rail, but hold the glued part in position for a minute to make sure that it has adhered.

Design two

This is a fun idea, with two teddies holding the half curtain.
The curtains are gathered onto wooden rails and edged with lace.
The top rail is finished with transparent beads.

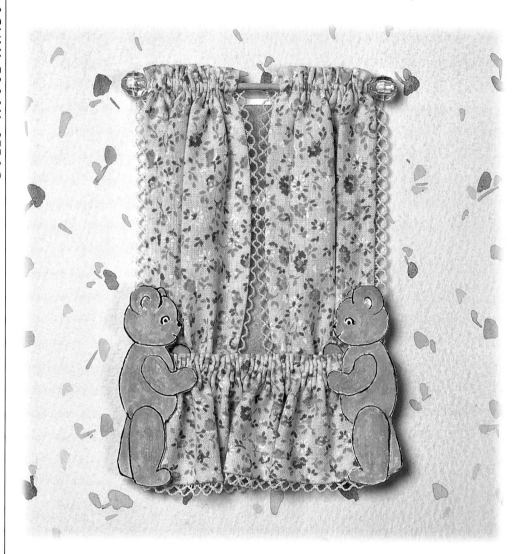

Materials

Window pattern
  and prepared
  polystyrene tile
Fabric
Lace trimming
Needle and thread
Scissors
Fabric stiffener
  (optional)
Dowel
Large-holed
  beads x 2
Stick adhesive
Tacky glue
Paper
Sharp pencil
Fairly stiff card
Watercolour, water-
  soluble crayon or
  felt-tip pen

METHOD

1 Trace the teddy drawings onto paper. Cut these out roughly and glue the pieces onto the card, using stick adhesive. Paint or otherwise colour the teddies, including the separate paws. Set aside to dry.

2 Cut out the fabric for the curtains, allowing for any turnings. Cut enough fabric for the finished half curtain to hang from the shoulder height of the teddies, down to their feet.

3 Make the three curtains following Method two under Gathering in Chapter 3 (see page 16). Finish each curtain with lace trimming as shown above.

You may want to use double fabric for the long curtains to present a finished view from the outside of your dolls' house. If so, sandwich the trimming between the two pieces of fabric.

4 Cut out the teddies and the two loose paws.

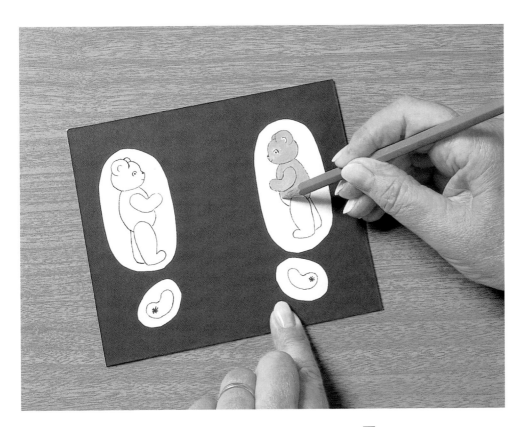

Colouring the
teddy outlines

5 Use tacky glue to fix a teddy over each end of the half curtain. Leave to dry.

6 Put a generous dab of tacky glue on the joining points of the loose paws and attach them behind the curtain so that the top of the paws can be seen (see the photo, left).

7 Tacky glue the half curtain to the other two curtains so the teddies' feet reach the windowsill.

8 Place a bead on each end of the top rail as a finishing touch.

9 Fix to the window in your chosen way.

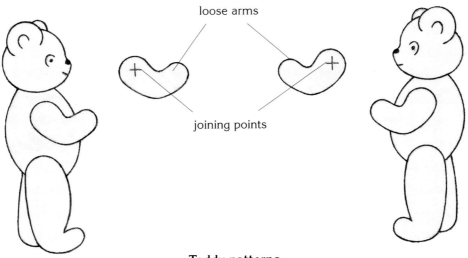

loose arms

joining points

Teddy patterns

PLAYROOMS AND BEDROOMS

*I enjoyed working on these designs. As I used checked fabric for each,
the cutting lines were already made, so I just counted the squares.*

Design one

*This has a gingham look and is bright and airy – I visualized a
bedspread to match. I made this blind following a different method
from the previous examples; I used a card base which meant combining
the two fabrics was more straightforward.*

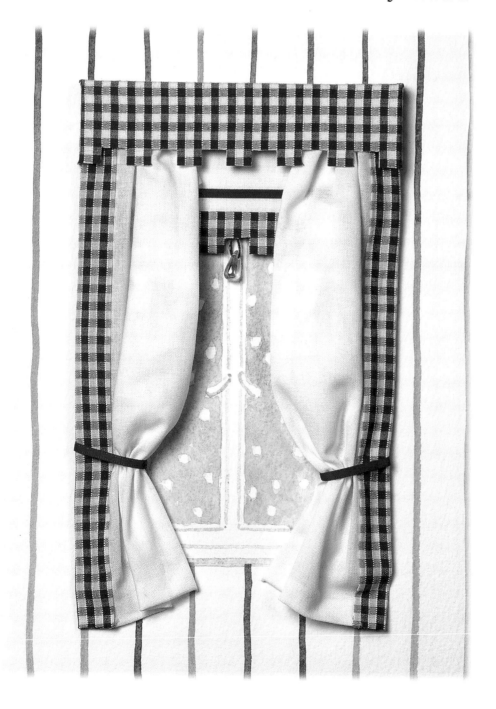

Materials

*Window pattern
and prepared
polystyrene tile
Card
Fabrics x 2
(1 check, 1 plain)
Pencil
Ruler
Scissors
Stick adhesive
Tacky glue
Ribbon trim
Dry iron
Needle and thread
Bead*

METHOD

PELMET

1 Design the pelmet to suit your fabric.

2 Draw the pelmet shape on card, following the instructions given under Basic pelmet in Chapter 4 (see page 34). Make the pattern quite deep to allow for cut-away shaping.

3 Spread the stick adhesive over the card, right to the edges, and press on the fabric, carefully lining up the squares with the edges of the card (see A in the photo below).

4 Trim the bottom edge level with the card and cut away the top corners. Glue down the overlapping edges (see B in the photo below).

5 Decide how deep you want the pelmet and cut away the excess fabric and card. Working from the centre, plan where the cuts for the crenellations will be, according to the pattern of squares. Cut out the crenellations and fold over the top and sides of the pelmet at the score lines (see C in the photo below).

6 Secure the corners of the pelmet with tacky glue and, if necessary, add small pieces of folded card to help hold the corners together (see Basic pelmet in Chapter 4, page 34).

BLIND

1 Cut the card to the same width as the inside of the pelmet and as deep as you wish, adding a little at the top (to keep in scale with the rest of your treatment) for folding over. Draw a line where this fold will be and score the card.

2 To make sure that the blind looks good from the outside of a dolls' house, use the plain fabric to cover the back as well as the front of the card, leaving 5mm (¼in) fold at the top (or other scale measurement). Trim the sides of the fabric to fit the card exactly (see A in the photo on page 102).

3 Fold down the top of the card at the score line (see B in the photo, over).

4 Cut a piece of checked fabric two-thirds the depth of the card (see C in the photo, over).

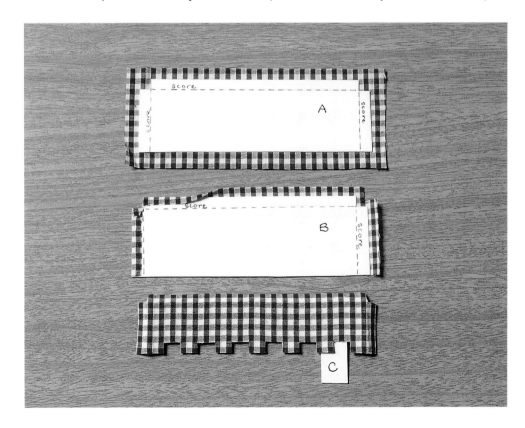

Covering the card for the pelmet

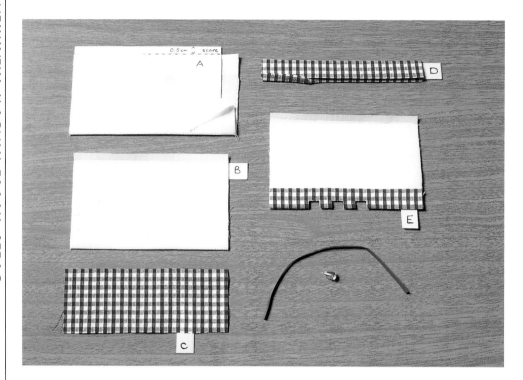

Covering the card for the blind

5 Fold over and press the long edges of this piece of fabric, then fold in half and press (see D in the photo above).

6 Place the lower part of the covered card inside the folded piece so that the checked material forms a strip along the bottom. Secure with stick adhesive.

7 Snip out the crenellations as you did for the pelmet (see E in the photo above).

8 If necessary, apply a little diluted tacky glue to the raw edges of the pelmet and blind to keep them from fraying.

9 Glue a thin ribbon to the blind, just above the crenellated bottom strip.

10 Finish with a bead-and-thread pull.

CURTAINS AND ASSEMBLY

1 Make the curtains according to your chosen method and glue the tops to the inside of the pelmet. I gathered the curtains and added ribbon tiebacks.

2 Glue the folded top of the blind to the inside top of the pelmet, behind the curtains.

Design two

This second idea is a little out of the ordinary. It doesn't have curtains as such, just 'hangings', one of which has storage pockets for playthings. The clown-and-star motifs are self-adhesive stickers which could be repeated elsewhere in the playroom.

Materials

Window pattern
  and prepared
  polystyrene tile
Card
Fabrics x 2
  (1 checked, 1 plain)
Scissors
Dry iron
Needle and thread
Stick adhesive
Tacky glue
Trimming
Self-adhesive stickers
  (clowns and stars)
Tiny toys etc

METHOD

PELMET AND BLIND

1 Cut out the card for the pelmet and the blind following the instructions given for Design one (see page 101), but do not allow any extra for shaping.

2 Cover both pieces of card with plain fabric. As for Design one, cover the back and front of the blind so that it looks good from the inside and outside of the window.

3 Add the trimming to the pelmet and blind, and finish the blind with a pull. For the treatment shown I stuck an adhesive star to a short length of ribbon.

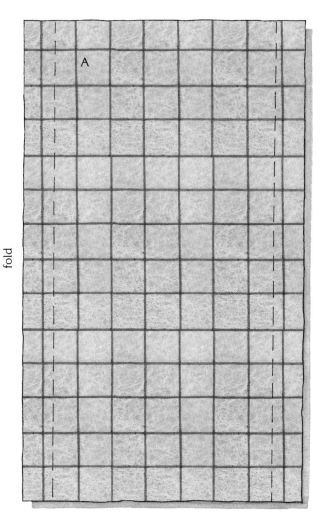

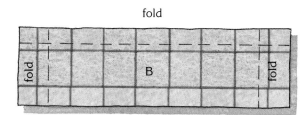

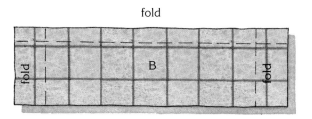

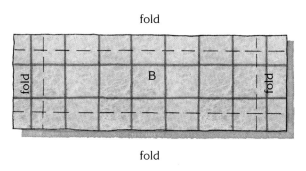

bottom pocket

Patterns and fold lines for pocket curtains

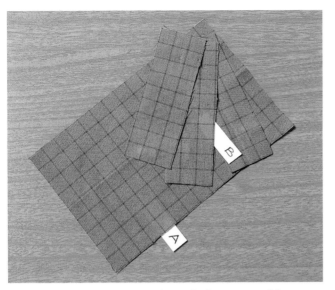

The fabric pieces cut and ready for assembly

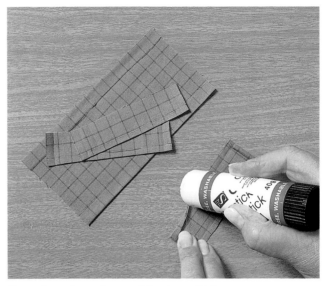

Securing the edges with glue stick

Pressing the edges of the fabric pieces

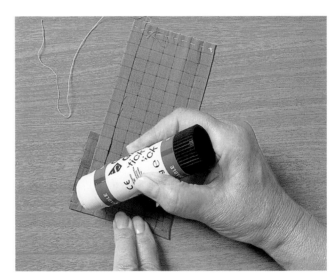

Gluing the pockets in place

CURTAINS

1 Cut the fabric for the 'pocket curtain', following the patterns for A and B opposite.

2 Cut the fabric for the narrow curtain to your own specifications. You may prefer to make an ordinary curtain here, or even another pocket one.

3 Fold over the edges of the pieces A and B as indicated opposite, and press with the iron.

4 Fix the side folds on piece A and the top edges of the pockets, B, using the stick adhesive, as shown top right.

5 Run a gathering thread through the top of the curtain, but do not pull it in yet.

6 Position the pockets on the curtain and fix them in place with stick adhesive.

7 Attach the narrow curtain to the back of the pelmet.

8 Pull up the gathers of the pocket curtain and assemble the window treatment as for Design one.

9 Add any final trims and stickers to the pelmet and curtains, then pop some playthings in the pockets.

8

EXTERNAL FEATURES

DORMER WINDOWS

Dormer windows, projecting from sloping roofs, provide some interesting challenges in terms of window treatments.

For a dolls' house

Dormer windows look attractive from the outside, but when the roof is lifted up to reveal the rooms beneath, the windows disappear – they end up upside down. What we need then, is to go for an outside view which is compatible with the room inside.

My design features a layered blind that is made from co-ordinated fabrics and trimmings. The back is plain.

Materials

Window pattern and prepared polystyrene tile
Fabrics x 2
Scissors
Thin card
Dowel
Fabric stiffener (optional)
Lace trimming
Embroidery cotton
Stick adhesive
Tacky glue
Needle and thread
Bead

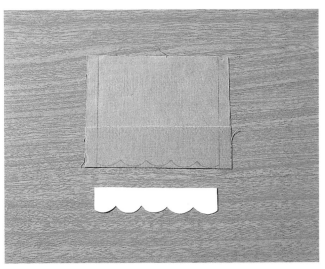
Using a template to trace on the scalloped edge

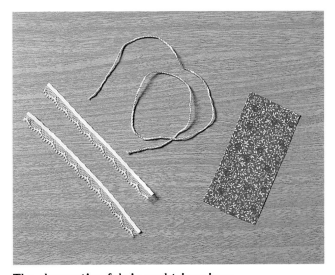
The decorative fabric and trimmings

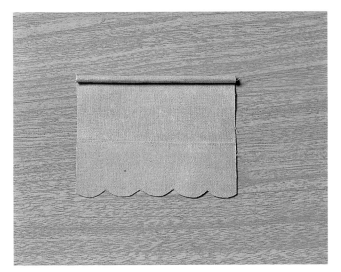
The shaped blind, with dowel attached

Using the template to position the trimmings

METHOD

1 Cut out and prepare the material for the blind, following the instructions given for Roller blinds in Chapter 4 (see page 29).

2 Cut out a card template with a scalloped edge (or in the shape of your choice), to the same width as the window. Trace around it onto the fabric prepared for the blind.

3 Trim the fabric to the width of the window and cut around the shaped edge. Attach a piece of dowel to the top, roll it over a couple of times, then glue it down with tacky glue.

4 Prepare the decorative piece of fabric and the trimmings, turning up a hem along one edge of the fabric.

5 Glue this second piece of fabric and the trimmings to the prepared blind, using either tacky glue or stick adhesive; use the template as a guide to fix the trimming along the scalloped edge.

6 Finish the blind with a bead-and-thread pull.

7 Apply a line of tacky glue across the blind at the top and a short way down each side, and fix in position on the window surround.

For a room box

A room box with a dormer window could be a studio bedroom or a loft conversion with a window at the back, which lends itself to a window treatment. A simple pair of curtains could be hung from a wooden rail or a specially made brass rail which fits between the walls of the dormer. This design, using a pipe cleaner, is very simple and follows a line around the inside of the window.

METHOD

1 Make a window pattern to fit around the inside of your dormer window. Lay the pattern out flat and place it between the two clingfilm layers of the polytile tool. This gives you a secure template to work with.

2 Design the curtains and prepare the fabric in your chosen way. I used the gathering method for the curtains shown.

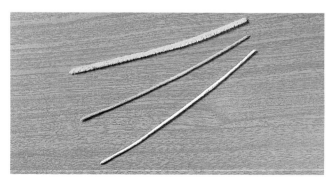

Top to bottom: the pipe cleaner untreated, coated with glue, and coloured

Materials

Window pattern
  and prepared
  polystyrene tile
Fabric
Scissors
Fabric stiffener
  (optional)
Pipe cleaner
Stick adhesive
Tacky glue
Paper
Damp cloth
Acrylic or emulsion
  paint with
  applicator
Decorative beads or
  findings x 2

The finished curtains with paper strips attached

3 Put dabs of tacky glue on the whole length of the pipe cleaner and run your finger and thumb along it to flatten the tufts. Keep doing this until the glue is dry – and have the damp cloth handy for wiping your fingers.

4 When the glue has set hard, coat the pipe cleaner with acrylic or emulsion paint in the colour of your choice. Set aside to dry.

5 When the curtains are ready, glue a strip of paper to the inside top of each one. This makes it easier to attach them to the pipe cleaner.

6 Use tacky glue to stick the curtains to the flat pipe cleaner, and when everything is completely dry, bend the pipe cleaner to fit the inside of the dormer window. Add a bead or finding to each end.

7 Use tacky glue to fix the curtain in place.

Gluing the curtains to the pipe cleaner

SHUTTERS

Shutters, known as brise-soleil in Mediterranean countries, are used
to protect windows from adverse weather conditions. They can be
positioned inside or outside a window. In stately Georgian homes
shutters were fixed inside the windows, to be drawn across
as protection against the sun or draughts and for privacy after dark.

This is a simple outside window cover which could be made from
mount card, balsa or obeche; if you use balsa choose a firm one, as
some can be rather soft and crumbly. I used obeche for these shutters.

Open shutters
Very simple shutters, positioned outside the window, had to be
closed from the outside, and were used as protection against wind
and rain. They were sometimes all that very poor dwellings
had to protect their occupants from the elements.

Materials

(for both designs)
Window pattern
Card, balsa or obeche
Modelling knife
Cutting board
Sharp pencil
Ruler
Paint (I used poster
  colours) and brush
Tacky glue
Cocktail sticks x 4
Clear, fast-dry enamel
  and brush

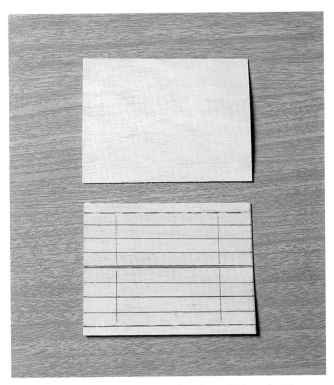

Marking on the outlines and joins of the shutters

METHOD

1 Measure the outside of the window, then cut your chosen material to the size of the whole window.

2 Mark the outline for both shutters on this one piece. With a sharp pencil, mark in all the lines to indicate the joins in the 'wood', starting with the centre line.

3 With the modelling knife, cut through the piece down the centre line and down one strip from each side for the jambs. These will be used as supports at the hinged side of the shutters.

4 Cut four strips from the card, balsa or obeche, slightly shorter than the remaining shutter width, for the cross pieces.

5 Paint all these pieces back and front, even though only one side will be on view: card, balsa and obeche will all curl when they are painted, but will straighten out again when painted on the other side.

6 Glue the cross pieces and jambs in position when the paint is dry.

7 Cut and paint tiny pieces of cocktail stick for hinges, and glue them in place as shown in the photo on page 115.

8 Glue the edges of the shutters to the jambs, with a slight overlap.

9 Give the finished shutters a thin coat of fast-dry enamel, being careful to remove any traces of 'trapped' enamel from around all the joins.

10 When the finishing coat is dry attach the shutters, by their jambs, to the outer sides of the window frame, with tacky glue.

Painting all the shutter pieces

Closed shutters

This very basic idea could easily be adapted to produce something more elaborate, with shaped hinges and decorative patterns.

METHOD

1 Follow steps 1 and 2 as for open shutters.

2 With the sharp pencil, redraw the line down the centre of the piece and each line where the shutters meet the jambs to make them slightly deeper than the lines indicating the joins in the wood.

3 Paint the complete piece front and back, to prevent it from curling.

4 Cut up the cocktail sticks to make hinges and handles; use the pointed ends as shown in the photo opposite. Paint them black and glue in position when dry.

5 Give the finished shutters a very thin coat of clear, fast-dry enamel. Again, be sure to remove any traces of 'trapped' enamel from around the hinges and handles.

6 Attach the shutters to your window in the way most appropriate to your setting.

If you're making an outdoor scene with closed shutters on a dummy wall, you won't need a window frame underneath. The shutters could be glued straight to the wall.

The tools and materials for making the hinges and handles

Cutting off the pointed ends of cocktail sticks for the hinges

VICTORIAN BAY WINDOW

The treatment of these three windows combines some of the techniques described in this book. The rather heavy appearance of the curtains was fairly typical of the Victorian era, when rooms were over-furnished and the daylight entering them was kept to a minimum.

PRACTICAL NOTES

I formed the curtains at the central window over shaped white card. This doesn't look too obvious as the net has quite a dense pattern; the gathering at the 'waist' helps to further obscure the card. A piece of matching single net runs across the curtains to about halfway down the window.

All of the curtains are based on the patterns for the double Victorian curtains in Chapter 5 (see page 64). However, the central set has coloured fabric at the back only, as the front parts are all net. The heading is a lambrequin, again based on the pattern given for the

Victorian curtains in Chapter 5 (see page 65). It has gold beads attached to each of its points to match the ends of the tiebacks. The advantage of using double fabric for the curtains is evident in this external view.

This design may look complicated, but it is not difficult to make. The only sewing involved is for gathering the curtains, as the whole treatment is glued together using tacky glue. I allowed drying time between each stage so that the individual sections weren't disturbed as I assembled them.

The finished sets of curtains were glued straight to the window frames, eliminating the need for a curtain rail.

9

DARING DESIGNS

REGENCY-STYLE CURTAINS

This design combines velvet, cotton and sheer nylon fabric
(anachronistic, and not for the purist maybe). The top is padded
and embellished with wire and floral decorations.
The florets are repeated as curtain tiebacks.

Materials

*Window pattern
  and prepared
  polystyrene tile
Fabrics x 3
Trimmings and
  embellishments
Soft, absorbent paper
  (eg kitchen towel)
Scissors
Needle and thread
Tacky glue
Paper strips*

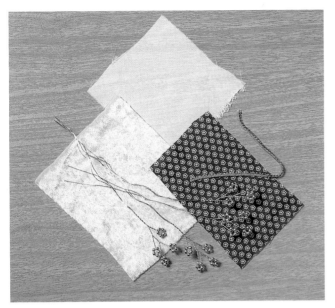

Regency-style materials

Forming the paper roll

METHOD

1 Trim the absorbent paper to the same width as the window. Roll it up and secure the roll with dabs of tacky glue.

2 Cut a piece of the main fabric (velvet in the treatment shown here) to fit around this roll, allowing for an overlap at each end. Turn the ends under and stitch or glue in place.

 Velvet is not always happy when glued and I found that stitching was more successful here.

3 Make the outer, velvet curtains in your chosen way.

4 Add the embellishments to the top roll, securing them in the most appropriate way for your choice of findings.

Stitching in the ends of the velvet covering

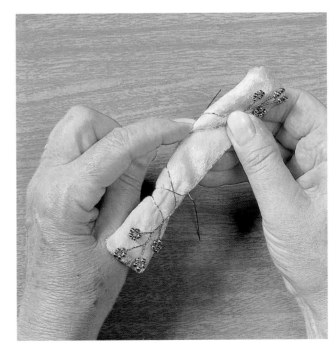

Adding the embellishments

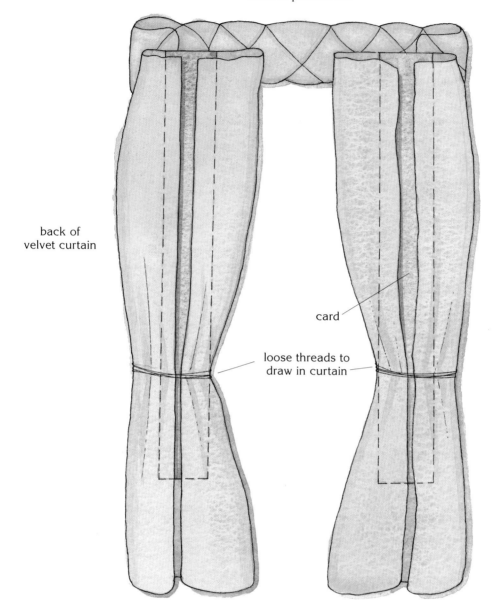

back of padded roll

back of
velvet curtain

card

loose threads to
draw in curtain

Joining the curtains to the top roll

5 Cut two narrow strips of paper and glue one across the top of each curtain, at the front. Join the curtains to the top roll by gluing their paper strips to it; this will give better adhesion than gluing fabric to fabric.

6 Cut the fabric for the central curtains, which are just straight pieces of doubled fabric with the hems turned up, and attach them to the back of the outer curtains, again using paper strips for better adhesion.

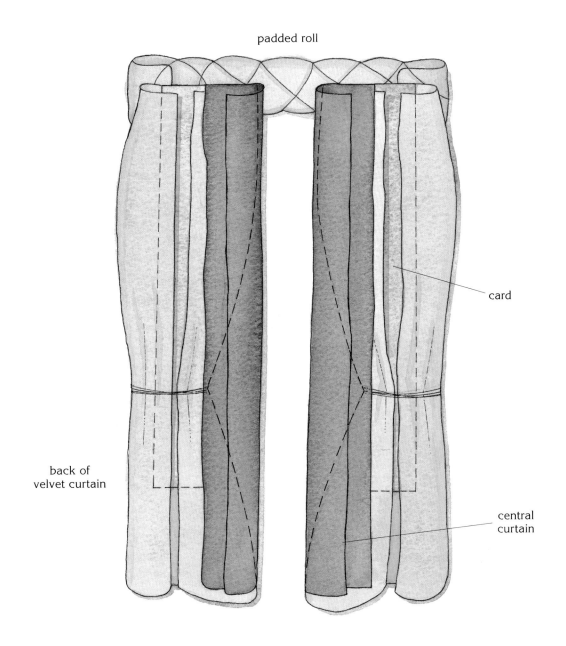

padded roll

card

back of
velvet curtain

central
curtain

Attaching the central curtains

7 Cut out the nylon for the sheer curtains, making them wide enough to meet in the middle. Again, these curtains are just straight pieces of fabric.

 I glued trimming along the edges of the sheer curtains to neaten and tone them in with the other curtains.

8 Attach these curtains to the back of the others, using strips of paper for better bonding.

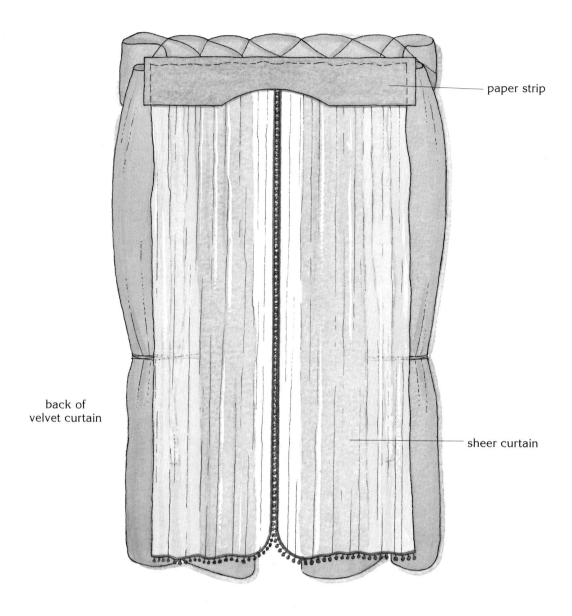

paper strip

back of
velvet curtain

sheer curtain

Attaching the sheer curtains

CHERUB-AND-PEARL PELMET AND CURTAINS

This design has cherubs watching over the room from their elevated position – not to everyone's taste. Most of the resources are similar to those for the previous design, with the exception of the absorbent paper.

Materials

Window pattern
  and prepared
  polystyrene tile
Fabric
Scissors
Needle and thread
Trimming
Firm card
Large, over-the
  -top motif
Paper
Extravagant
  trimmings
Tacky glue

METHOD

1 Make the pelmet following the instructions for Basic pelmet in Chapter 4 (see page 34).

2 Add the exaggerated ornamentation and trimming to the pelmet. I used tacky glue for this treatment but you could stitch it in place.

3 Make the curtains in your chosen way and attach them to the inside of the pelmet, using strips of paper to give better adhesion.

4 Put in a line of gathering stitches where the tiebacks will be, then add the tiebacks. For this set of curtains, I made the tiebacks from the trimming I used for the pelmet.

A NAUTICAL TOUCH

*This blind is pleated horizontally; it might hang at a window
in the room of a keen yachtsman.*

Materials

*Window pattern
 and prepared
 polystyrene tile
White cotton fabric
Scissors
Pleater and 'plastics'
Fabric stiffener
Hair dryer (optional)
White paper
 (optional)
Tacky glue
Needle and thread
Bead
Nautical decoration
Thin card*

METHOD

1 Cut the fabric to the width of the window and twice the length of the required drop.

2 Dampen the fabric and then apply the stiffening solution.

3 Turn up a small hem at the top and bottom before positioning the curtain on the pleater, and working in the grooves.

4 Dry the fabric with the hair dryer, or set the work aside to dry naturally.

5 When the pleated fabric is completely dry, remove it from the pleater, being careful to preserve the pleats.

6 Cut a piece of paper to the exact size of the pleated fabric. Run a line of tacky glue around the edges of the paper and carefully attach the fabric to it. Try not to squash the pleats.

 This paper isn't essential, but it does help to firm up the blind.

7 Make a pull from the bead and thread, and stitch it in place.

8 Cut a piece of card to back the nautical decoration. This should be straight at the sides and bottom, but should follow the outline of the decoration across the top (as shown in the photo). Glue the decoration to the card, then glue the whole assembly to the top of the blind.

BLACK-AND-GOLD CURTAINS

For this design I used gilt metallic mesh combined with firm, black-and-gold, velvet ribbon which was stiffened with wire along the edges. The effect is rather avant-garde. This treatment looks good in a room which has a mainly black-and-gold theme, and a big window.

Materials

*Window pattern
    and prepared
    polystyrene tile
Firm card
Gold mesh
Stiffened velvet
    ribbon
Scissors
Gold tassels x 2
Decorative hair
    slides x 2
Tacky glue*

METHOD

1 Make the pelmet following the instructions for Basic pelmet in Chapter 4 (see page 34). Cover it with velvet ribbon, trimming to fit.

2 For each curtain, join two pieces of ribbon together along their length so that they are wide enough to bunch up a little: wired velvet is too 'strong' to be gathered.

3 Glue strips of firm card to the front of the ribbons, at the top, before attaching them to the inside of the pelmet. This card will hold the gathers in place – without it you will not get a secure bond.

4 Cut the inner mesh curtains to fit across the window, plus a little extra for the draped effect.

5 'Tie back' the mesh curtains with a pair of decorative hair slides, then attach them behind the velvet ribbon curtains, again using strips of card for better bonding.

6 Fix a gold tassel to each side of the pelmet.

SOFT SPOTS PELMET AND CURTAINS

This design is self-explanatory; you just need your window measurements and some ideas on helpful basic resources. Follow the basic methods given in Chapters 3 and 4.

PRACTICAL NOTES

I used very soft velvet for this design and found it easy to drape, but it does need strips of thin card to bond the curtains to the pelmet as in the previous designs. I made a pelmet with deep sides and soft tiebacks. This window treatment might be partnered with matching throws and cushions in a safari-themed room with pictures of animals.

THE BOUDOIR

As for the previous curtain, this design follows the basic methods given in Chapters 3 and 4; just find your window measurements, and use what materials you have available.

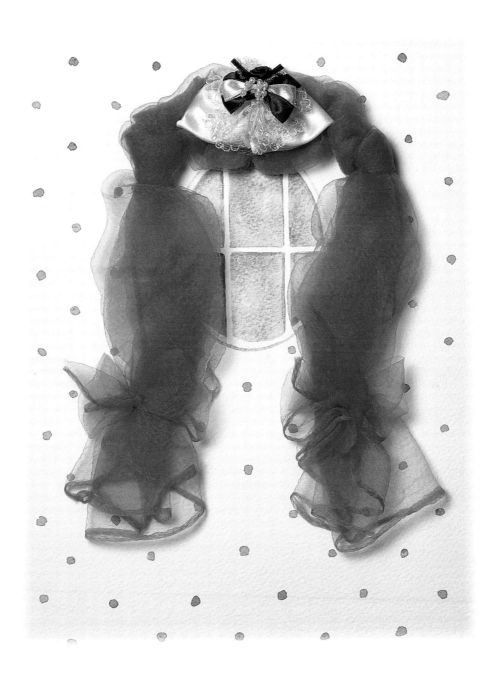

PRACTICAL NOTES

I used a chiffon scarf bought from a charity stall. Using the whole scarf made quite a large pair of curtains best suited to a big window; use just as much as you need.

I cut off two pieces to make the bow tie-backs, then gathered up the rest, knotted and bunched it. I finished the curtains by gluing an extremely elaborate hairclip to the top. Very bouffant. Ideal for the lady with rather down-market tastes.

GLOSSARY

Art Deco decorative style of the 1920s and 1930s, at its height in the 1930s

bay an angular window which projects from a house, giving three aspects of view and having a flat or sloping roof

bow a bay window that is curved

came thin lead strip securing the panes in a stained glass window

casement window frame hinged down one side

curtain lengths of cloth fabric hung at the window to act as a screen

dormer a projecting upright window in a sloping roof

dowel a cylindrical wooden rod

eclectic a mixture of styles drawn from different sources

Edwardian the popular style during the period between 1901 and 1910 when Edward, the eldest son of Queen Victoria and Prince Albert, was the reigning king of England

glazed windows glass-paned windows

jamb the side post of a window or doorway

lambrequin pronounced 'lamperkin', this term originally referred to a short piece of drapery over a door or window. The term is now used to denote a shaped board covered with a flat piece of fabric

lights glass window panes

mullion the upright dividing bar or strip between the panes of a window

oriel a projecting window in an upper storey, supported on wooden or masonry brackets

pelmet a narrow border of cloth or wood fitted above a window to conceal the curtain rail

polystyrene a polymer of foamed plastic

Regency the period between 1811 and 1820, when the future King George IV of England became Regent. The Prince Regent's best memorial is the Brighton Pavilion

rickrack zigzag braid for trimming

sash a window consisting of two sliding frames set in grooves in a fixed window frame

sheers very fine, light, delicate, fabrics that are almost transparent

shutter a screen over a window

swag a long fabric panel attached above the window, either to a pelmet or to the curtain rail

template a flat piece of wood, metal or card used as a guide to draw a desired shape

tieback a decorative length of fabric or trimming used to hold back a curtain to give a draped effect

transom horizontal bar dividing a window

transom window the window set above a transom bar

valance a short, decorative fabric arrangement placed at the top of a window

Victorian the period between 1837 and 1901 when Victoria was the reigning monarch, with Prince Albert as her consort

ABOUT THE AUTHOR

Eve Harwood became interested in
miniatures just before her retirement from the
Education Service, in 1995, following 30 years
in this varied and challenging career. She is
now chairman of the Cheshire Miniaturists' Club
and sells her own work, trading as
Chateau d'un Designs. Her handcrafted
miniatures have been sold both at fairs and
through commissions. Eve's double garage is
home to her miniature tools and resources,
leaving very little room for the cars.

She has three dolls' houses which are
mainly finished with collectors' items but has
many room boxes, each made and styled to
her own designs. She gives talks and
demonstrations to charitable organizations
and miniaturists' clubs.

INDEX

TITLES AVAILABLE FROM
GMC PUBLICATIONS
BOOKS

WOODCARVING

The Art of the Woodcarver	*GMC Publications*
Beginning Woodcarving	*GMC Publications*
Carving Architectural Detail in Wood: The Classical Tradition	
	Frederick Wilbur
Carving Birds & Beasts	*GMC Publications*
Carving the Human Figure: Studies in Wood and Stone	
	Dick Onians
Carving Nature: Wildlife Studies in Wood	*Frank Fox-Wilson*
Carving Realistic Birds	*David Tippey*
Decorative Woodcarving	*Jeremy Williams*
Elements of Woodcarving	*Chris Pye*
Essential Woodcarving Techniques	*Dick Onians*
Lettercarving in Wood: A Practical Course	*Chris Pye*
Making & Using Working Drawings for Realistic Model Animals	
	Basil F. Fordham
Power Tools for Woodcarving	*David Tippey*
Relief Carving in Wood: A Practical Introduction	*Chris Pye*
Understanding Woodcarving	*GMC Publications*
Understanding Woodcarving in the Round	*GMC Publications*
Useful Techniques for Woodcarvers	*GMC Publications*
Wildfowl Carving – Volume 1	*Jim Pearce*
Wildfowl Carving – Volume 2	*Jim Pearce*
Woodcarving: A Complete Course	*Ron Butterfield*
Woodcarving: A Foundation Course	*Zoë Gertner*
Woodcarving for Beginners	*GMC Publications*
Woodcarving Tools & Equipment Test Reports	*GMC Publications*
Woodcarving Tools, Materials & Equipment	*Chris Pye*

WOODTURNING

Adventures in Woodturning	*David Springett*
Bert Marsh: Woodturner	*Bert Marsh*
Bowl Turning Techniques Masterclass	*Tony Boase*
Colouring Techniques for Woodturners	*Jan Sanders*
Contemporary Turned Wood: New Perspectives in a Rich Tradition	*Ray Leier, Jan Peters & Kevin Wallace*
The Craftsman Woodturner	*Peter Child*
Decorating Turned Wood: The Maker's Eye	
	Liz & Michael O'Donnell
Decorative Techniques for Woodturners	*Hilary Bowen*
Fun at the Lathe	*R.C. Bell*
Illustrated Woodturning Techniques	*John Hunnex*
Intermediate Woodturning Projects	*GMC Publications*
Keith Rowley's Woodturning Projects	*Keith Rowley*
Making Screw Threads in Wood	*Fred Holder*
Turned Boxes: 50 Designs	*Chris Stott*
Turning Green Wood	*Michael O'Donnell*
Turning Miniatures in Wood	*John Sainsbury*
Turning Pens and Pencils	*Kip Christensen & Rex Burningham*
Understanding Woodturning	*Ann & Bob Phillips*
Useful Techniques for Woodturners	*GMC Publications*
Useful Woodturning Projects	*GMC Publications*

Woodturning: Bowls, Platters, Hollow Forms, Vases, Vessels, Bottles, Flasks, Tankards, Plates	*GMC Publications*
Woodturning: A Foundation Course (New Edition)	*Keith Rowley*
Woodturning: A Fresh Approach	*Robert Chapman*
Woodturning: An Individual Approach	*Dave Regester*
Woodturning: A Source Book of Shapes	*John Hunnex*
Woodturning Jewellery	*Hilary Bowen*
Woodturning Masterclass	*Tony Boase*
Woodturning Techniques	*GMC Publications*
Woodturning Tools & Equipment Test Reports	*GMC Publications*
Woodturning Wizardry	*David Springett*

WOODWORKING

Advanced Scrollsaw Projects	*GMC Publications*
Beginning Picture Marquetry	*Lawrence Threadgold*
Bird Boxes and Feeders for the Garden	*Dave Mackenzie*
Complete Woodfinishing	*Ian Hosker*
David Charlesworth's Furniture-Making Techniques	
	David Charlesworth
David Charlesworth's Furniture-Making Techniques – Volume 2	
	David Charlesworth
The Encyclopedia of Joint Making	*Terrie Noll*
Furniture-Making Projects for the Wood Craftsman	
	GMC Publications
Furniture-Making Techniques for the Wood Craftsman	
	GMC Publications
Furniture Projects	*Rod Wales*
Furniture Restoration (Practical Crafts)	*Kevin Jan Bonner*
Furniture Restoration: A Professional at Work	*John Lloyd*
Furniture Restoration and Repair for Beginners	*Kevin Jan Bonner*
Furniture Restoration Workshop	*Kevin Jan Bonner*
Green Woodwork	*Mike Abbott*
The History of Furniture	*Michael Huntley*
Intarsia: 30 Patterns for the Scrollsaw	*John Everett*
Kevin Ley's Furniture Projects	*Kevin Ley*
Making & Modifying Woodworking Tools	*Jim Kingshott*
Making Chairs and Tables	*GMC Publications*
Making Chairs and Tables – Volume 2	*GMC Publications*
Making Classic English Furniture	*Paul Richardson*
Making Heirloom Boxes	*Peter Lloyd*
Making Little Boxes from Wood	*John Bennett*
Making Screw Threads in Wood	*Fred Holder*
Making Shaker Furniture	*Barry Jackson*
Making Woodwork Aids and Devices	*Robert Wearing*
Mastering the Router	*Ron Fox*
Minidrill: Fifteen Projects	*John Everett*
Pine Furniture Projects for the Home	*Dave Mackenzie*
Practical Scrollsaw Patterns	*John Everett*
Router Magic: Jigs, Fixtures and Tricks to Unleash your Router's Full Potential	*Bill Hylton*
Router Tips & Techniques	*GMC Publications*
Routing: A Workshop Handbook	*Anthony Bailey*
Routing for Beginners	*Anthony Bailey*

UPHOLSTERY

TOYMAKING

DOLLS' HOUSES AND MINIATURES

CRAFTS

GARDENING

PHOTOGRAPHY

VIDEOS

MAGAZINES

WOODTURNING ◆ WOODCARVING

FURNITURE & CABINETMAKING

THE ROUTER ◆ WOODWORKING

THE DOLLS' HOUSE MAGAZINE

WATER GARDENING

BLACK & WHITE PHOTOGRAPHY

OUTDOOR PHOTOGRAPHY

BUSINESSMATTERS

The above represents a full list of all titles currently published or scheduled to be published.
All are available direct from the Publishers or through bookshops, newsagents and specialist retailers.
To place an order, or to obtain a complete catalogue, contact:

GMC Publications,
Castle Place, 166 High Street, Lewes, East Sussex BN7 1XU, United Kingdom
Tel: 01273 488005 Fax: 01273 478606
E-mail: pubs@thegmcgroup.com
Orders by credit card are accepted